"Beware of avarice; it is a bad and incurable disease."

EGYPTIAN PROVERB, C. 2400 B.C.

"Money has never yet made anyone rich."

SENECA, STOIC PHILOSOPHER, 1ST CENTURY

"Nothing that is God's is obtainable by money."

TERTULLIAN, CHRISTIAN THEOLOGIAN, 3RD CENTURY

"Lives based on having are less free than lives based on doing or being."

WILLIAM JAMES, PHILOSOPHER OF PRAGMATISM, EARLY 20TH CENTURY

"It is preoccupation with possessions, more than anything else, that prevents persons from living freely and nobly."

BERTRAND RUSSELL, PHILOSOPHER OF LOGIC, EARLY 20TH CENTURY

"We make a living by what we get; we make a life by what we give."

SIR WINSTON CHURCHILL, ENGLISH STATESMAN, MID-20TH CENTURY

"If a person gets his attitude toward money right, it will straighten out almost every other area in his life."

BILLY GRAHAM, CHRISTIAN EVANGELIST, LATE 20TH CENTURY

Giving to God

The Bible's Good News
about Living a Generous Life

Mark Allan Powell

WILLIAM B. EERDMANS PUBLISHING COMPANY
GRAND RAPIDS, MICHIGAN / CAMBRIDGE, U.K.

WM. B. EERDMANS PUBLISHING CO.
2140 Oak Industrial Drive N.E., Grand Rapids, Michigan 49505 /
P.O. Box 163, Cambridge CB3 9PU U.K.

Text design by Kevin van der Leek Design Inc.
Set in Arnhem and Sansa

Printed in the United States of America

17 16 15 14 13 12   14 13 12 11 10 9

Library of Congress Cataloging-in-Publication Data

Powell, Mark Allan, 1953 –
    Giving to God: the Bible's good news about living a generous life /
Mark Allan Powell.
        p.   cm.
    ISBN 978-0-8028-2926-9
    (pbk.: alk. paper)
            1. Christian giving.   I. Title.

BV772.P675 2006
248′.6 — dc22

                                        2005034139

www.eerdmans.com

For Cheryl K. Rinell
my sister

Contents

Acknowledgments

I HAVE DONE THE BEST I can to produce a guide to biblical stewardship that will be faithful to the teaching of Scripture, to the promises of Christ, and to the needs of those who view giving to God as an opportunity and expectation for their journey of faith. The book has been greatly improved, however, by the counsel of others. I sent an early draft of the manuscript to Dennis Anderson, Paul Fransen, Rick Barger, and Walter Taylor, ministers of the gospel and teachers of Scripture who graciously provided suggestions and advice. I thank them for the time they devoted to the project, and for their invaluable insights. I am grateful also to Trinity Lutheran Seminary for granting me the resources to pursue this study and for providing me with a community of faith in which academic scholarship and pastoral practice are always intertwined. Finally, I wish to thank Michael Thomson for steering me towards Eerdmans as a venue for publishing this project, and Andrew Hoogheem, my editor there, for his expertise in bringing it to fruition. All of these have been instrumental in transforming my thoughts and words into the physical product that you now hold in your hands.

Introduction:
Getting Completely Wet

Remember the Lord your God, for it is he who gives you power to get wealth.

Deuteronomy 8:18

HAVE YOU HEARD THE STORY about the baptism of the Gauls? It may not be historically factual, but this is not a history book, so we won't worry too much about that.

The Gauls were a warlike people who in ancient times inhabited what is now France and Belgium. They spoke a Celtic language and were Druidic by religion. By the time of the Christian era they had been conquered by the Roman Empire and were supposedly under its control. The extent of this control varied, however, for the Gauls never did take too well to being conquered and there were numerous Gallic uprisings.

A number of Christian missionaries ventured into Gallic territory and, over time, many of the Gauls became Christians. As the story goes, when a converted warrior was baptized in a river or stream, he would hold one arm high in the air as the missionary dunked him under the water. This seemed a peculiar custom and the missionaries soon learned the reason for it. When the next battle or skirmish broke out, the warlike Gaul could proclaim "This arm is not baptized!", grab up his club or sword or ax, and ride off to destroy his enemy in a most un-Christian manner.

As I've indicated, this story is probably not historically authentic. My guess is that it's a medieval version of what we would call an "urban legend" and I certainly do not intend to cast any aspersions on the Gauls or their descendants by repeating it. I just find the *image* so compelling: the picture of someone — anyone — trying to keep one part of their body, one aspect of their identity, free from the influence of baptism.

This book is about stewardship, and stewardship is about getting completely wet. It is about looking at ourselves, discovering what it is that we would like to keep dry, and then immersing whatever that is in the waters of Holy Baptism.

Stewardship is about giving to God. It is about turning total control of our lives over to God. It is about taking seriously the words that we so easily pray: "Thy kingdom come, thy will be done." When we pray, "Thy kingdom come," we ask God to rule our lives. When we pray, "Thy will be done," we ask for what God wants to happen in our lives to take place — already, now, on earth as in heaven.

But when you hear the word *stewardship,* what is the first thing that you think of?

Many people say, "Money," and there may be two different reasons for that. First, there is a lingering misconception among many Christians that stewardship is just a fancy word for "fund-raising." Churches are partly to blame for this because many churches refer to their annual fund appeal as a "stewardship campaign." But stewardship is not fund-raising. It is a way of life.

Still, there is another reason why people associate stewardship with money, and I think that this second reason is completely appropriate. In today's world, *money* is the one thing that many of us would most like to keep dry. I picture modern Christians going under the water with that outstretched arm clutching . . . not an ax or a war-hammer, but a purse or wallet. And *that* is why, when we talk about stewardship today, we often talk about money more than we do about anything else.

For some years now teachers in the church have been trying to get people to realize that stewardship is not *just* about money. Someone came up with the alliterative phrase "time, talents, and treasures." There is also the whole matter of "stewardship of the earth," taking proper care of the planet that God has given us (Genesis 1:26; Psalm 8:6): conserving water, recycling paper and aluminum, preserving wetlands and rainforests. And there is "stewardship of our bodies" (Romans 12:1; 1 Corinthians 6:19-20): getting exercise, eating right, managing stress, flossing our teeth. Or we might speak of "stewardship of our families" (Exodus 20:12; Proverbs 22:6; Mark 7:9-13; 1 Timothy 5:8): nurturing our marriages, raising happy and healthy children, caring for elderly parents. We might even speak of "stewardship of the gospel" (1 Corinthians 4:1; 9:16-17; 2 Corinthians 5:18-20; 1 Peter 4:10): preserving the life-giving message of what God has done through Jesus

🖋 What Is Stewardship? Some Sample Definitions

"Christian stewardship is the *practice* of the Christian religion. It is neither a department of life nor a sphere of activity. It is the Christian conception of life as a whole, manifested in attitudes and actions."

W. H. Greever (1937)

"Christian stewardship is the practice of systematic and proportionate giving of time, abilities, and material possessions, based upon the conviction that these are trusts from God to be used in his service for the benefit of all mankind in grateful acknowledgment of Christ's redeeming love."

National Council of Churches
United Stewardship Council (1946)

"Stewardship is what we do after we say we believe."

Clarence C. Stoughton (1949)

"Stewardship is partnership with Christ, through the Holy Spirit, in fulfilling the purposes of God in the world."

A. C. Conrad (1955)

"Stewardship is the re-enactment of Christ's life in Christ's people."

T. A. Kantonen (1956)

"Stewardship is the management of life and all its resources for God and for the good of all."

Robert Hastings (1961)

"Stewardship is receiving and sharing God's bounteous gifts and managing them for the best promotion of God's purposes in the world."

Milo Kauffman (1975)

"Stewardship is taking care of the bounty that God continually provides us."

L. David Brown (1978)

"Christian stewardship has come to mean 'what we do with what we have, all the time.'"

John H. MacNaughton (1983)

"Stewardship is a philosophy of life and a theological form of self-management."

John Brackett (1988)

"Stewardship is God's grace working God's purpose out in the world, in, with and through us, who, in grateful response to God and through faith in Jesus Christ, enter into a covenant relationship with the empowering Spirit of God that blesses all of creation."

Rhodes Thompson (1990)

Christ and sharing that message with the world. In truth, stewardship may involve lots of things.

Properly speaking, stewardship is about all of life, about giving ourselves to God and using all that God has given us in grateful and appropriate ways. Still, in this book we will talk about money more than anything else because I find that for many of us this is where the issues become most real.

The Bible reports Jesus as saying, "You cannot serve God and mammon" (Matthew 6:24, RSV; *mammon* refers to money and the things that money can buy — material possessions). Jesus might have said this about "God and politics" or about "God and sports" or about God and any number of other things that might become obsessions. But he didn't. He said, "God and mammon." *Money.*

The Bible also presents the apostle Paul as saying, "The love of money is the root of all kinds of evil" (1 Timothy 6:10). Paul might have said this about "the love of status" or "the love of power" or the love of any number of other things. But he didn't. He said *money.*

These biblical figures knew something that is still true today. Money and material possessions are especially prominent candidates for idolatry (Ephesians 5:5; Colossians 3:5), chief contenders for unwarranted affection. Martin Luther is reported to have said that humans need to experience three conversions: of heart and mind and purse. Even baptized people like to keep their money dry. In fact, many of us try to rope off this one area of our lives as "off-limits" to spiritual inspection. "It's nobody's business what I do with my money," we say, realizing too late just how foolish that sounds. It's God's business, isn't it? Of course it is.

But here is something that many people do not know: what the Bible teaches about stewardship is *good* news! When we come to understand and practice what the Bible says about stewardship, we will have happier, better lives.

The purpose of this book is to offer a biblical vision for financial stewardship, a vision that turns out to be filled with good news for followers of Jesus Christ. The vision is presented in two parts.

First, we will try to arrive at a better understanding of what stewardship means. Part One of this book presents stewardship as a joy-filled aspect of our relationship with God and describes giving to God as an act of worship, an expression of faith, and a discipline for spiritual growth. The overall focus is on understanding stewardship as a way of life, indeed as *the* way of life for people who belong to God.

Second, we will explore ways of being more faithful in our practice of financial stewardship. Part Two of this book moves beyond theoretical understanding to deal with pragmatic concerns, such as "How do I use all of my money in God-pleasing ways?" and "How much money should I give to the church?" The goal will be to address such questions in an appropriate and realistic way, taking into account both what the Bible says and the context and challenges of modern living. I try to lay out a program for living and giving that most Christians will be able to embrace as both a duty and a delight.

Discussion Questions

1. What do you think of when you hear the word *stewardship*? What positive or negative images come to mind?

2. The chart on pages xiv - xv offers some definitions of stewardship that Christian leaders have offered over the years. Which do you like the best? Why? Could you or your study group come up with a definition that would be better suited for your own church or congregation?

3. What does the author mean when he says that "baptized people like to keep their money dry" (page xvi)? Have you found this to be true in your life or in the lives of those you know?

PART ONE

Belonging to God

All things are yours . . . and you belong to Christ, and Christ belongs to God.

1 Corinthians 3:21-23

STEWARDSHIP IS NOT JUST A way of life; it is a *good* way
of life. In fact, for many, it is a way to a *better* life. Think of
it this way: stewardship means belonging to God. It means
allowing God to rule our lives, putting God in charge of
everything, including our time and our money. I can understand why that might sound threatening — surrendering
control does not come easily to any of us. But God is good
at ruling people's lives. If we really do belong to God and if
we really do put God in charge of everything, we will not be
the worse for it.

Of course, how this plays out in practice may be difficult to determine. Faithful
stewardship can be a struggle
and I don't want to give an
unrealistic, rosy picture that
suggests otherwise. Still, we
must begin with this basic vision: our goal is to find the life
that God wants us to have, in confidence that this will be
the best life we could possibly have.

🎵 **Our goal is to find
the life that God wants
us to have.**

Most of us know that the Bible contains a lot of commandments, a lot of dos and don'ts regarding how God
wants us to live. We also may know that quite a few of these
pertain to how we use our money and, even without seeing a list of those commandments, we may suspect that we
are not doing an adequate job of keeping them. Indeed,
we may remember that Jesus told some people to sell all
of their possessions and give the money to the poor and
we may have heard stories of special saints (like Francis of
Assisi) who did just that. We may figure that God's expectations for what we should do with our money are so high

that we will never be able to measure up. We are tempted to conclude that the best thing to do is avoid paying too much attention to this topic and just accept our imperfection with varying degrees of denial and discomfort.

What we might not realize is that the Bible also contains a great many *promises* regarding stewardship of time, talents, and treasures (especially treasures), promises designed to inspire our confidence rather than arouse our guilt. As is often the case, the teaching of the Bible includes both *law* and *gospel:* the law tells us what we are supposed to do for God while the gospel reveals what God does for us. We ought not ignore the "stewardship laws" of the Bible, but we should be even more concerned with learning the stewardship gospel, with understanding the broad concept of what it means to belong to God. And what *does* that mean? It means that we are in a relationship with a God who loves us, guides us, guards us, and blesses us.

What we are supposed to do for God is directly related to what God does for us. For example, the Bible teaches that generosity is a fruit of God's Holy Spirit (Galatians 5:22-23). The way to become generous people, then, involves not quenching God's Spirit (1 Thessalonians 5:19), but allowing the transforming work of Christ to have its full effect in shaping us to be the people God wants us to be (Romans 12:2; 2 Corinthians 5:17; Galatians 2:20; Philippians 1:6). Douglas John Hall, in his book entitled *The Steward,* puts it this way:

> The law of stewardship, which many know to be true
> enough, insists that human beings must be faithful

trustees of the life of the world. But it is one thing to know this and another to *do* it. The gospel of stewardship begins by overcoming that within us which prevents our being stewards — the pride of imagining ourselves owners; the sloth of irresponsibility, neglect, and apathy. And that gospel gives us the grace and courage that we need to exercise a love that is larger than our self-esteem or our anxiety about ourselves. (p. 44)

In this first section of this book we will look at stewardship as a joy-filled aspect of our relationship with God. We will not be primarily concerned with what we *should* do — whether we should give our money away, where we should give it, how we should give it, or how much we should give. These concerns will come up in Part Two of this book, but for now we are less interested in expectations or requirements than in understanding the good news of Scripture that makes giving to God something we will *want* to do.

This section of the book is divided into three chapters, devoted to various aspects of what stewardship can be:

First, faithful stewardship involves giving to God as an *act of worship.* We give out of glad and generous hearts as an expression of love and devotion to the God who is so good to us. When we do this, we discover the very essence of Christianity: a heartfelt relationship with God in which joy and thanksgiving replace self-interest or guilt.

Second, faithful stewardship involves giving to God as an *expression of our faith.* We confess that all we are and everything we have belongs to God and we put this faith into action when we offer ourselves and our possessions to God to be used as God sees fit. When we do this we discover the practical value of our faith: the God who creates, redeems, and sustains us is ready and willing to rule our lives and provide us with everything we need to be content.

Third, faithful stewardship involves giving to God as a *discipline for spiritual growth.* We practice a degree of renunciation and self-denial in recognition of the spiritual principle that "where your treasure is, there your heart will be also" (Matthew 6:21). When we do this we discover that such giving becomes a bond that brings us closer to God and helps us to become the sort of people we most want to be.

In each of these chapters, we will discover that giving is one way of participating in a relationship with the God who loves and cares for us, of enjoying a deep and satisfying relationship with the God to whom we belong. Understanding the good news of stewardship means discovering the way of life that the Bible calls "belonging to God."

Discussion Questions

1. Think about what it means to "belong to God": Do you find that concept threatening or promising? Can it be both at the same time?

2. Do you tend to regard "giving to the church" as something you *ought* to do or as something you *want* to do? What might have to happen for you to think of giving as more of an opportunity than an obligation?

3. What do you hope to get out of the next three chapters of this book? How would you complete the following sentences?

I would be disappointed if these chapters . . .

I would be delighted if these chapters . . .

CHAPTER ONE

An Act of Worship

All things come from you, and of your own have we given you.

1 Chronicles 29:14

PICTURE YOURSELF IN ANCIENT ISRAEL, in the early years before there was a temple. The community gathers to worship around some rudimentary altar and each person brings an offering to God. Some have "drink offerings" that they pour out on the altar un-

> 🐟 **The offering is an act of worship.**

til the liquid is gone. Others have grain offerings, sheaves of wheat that they place on the altar and light on fire. A few may even bring birds or small animals, which are killed and, like the wheat, consumed in the flames.

What is the point? Well, as any Old Testament commentary or encyclopedia will tell you, the thinking that justified such sacrificial rites could be varied and complex. But the *basic* point seems to have been this: worshipers brought things that they valued to the altar and left them there.

They gave them up; they gave them away. The liquid was poured out, the animals were slaughtered, the grain was incinerated. People gave offerings to God as an act of worship and those offerings were simply destroyed.

I wonder what would happen in a modern church if we collected the offering on Sunday morning, set the plates on the altar, and then tossed in a match, burning up everyone's money. Alright, I know that would be illegal — it is against the law to burn or destroy U.S. currency. I also realize that most people probably write checks, so for them it wouldn't really matter. But my point is that many people in modern congregations would be appalled if the offerings they gave to the church were simply destroyed rather than put to some good use. Of course, that only makes sense . . . but then what was going on in ancient Israel?

The grain, the animals, even the drink offerings . . . these were the ancient equivalents of money. The Israelites found it worthwhile, indeed necessary, to give away their possessions in sacrificial acts of worship to God. The point was not what happened to the grain after it was placed on the altar; the point was simply putting that grain on the altar in the first place.

I sometimes imagine someone in Israel saying, after a time, "You know, it is kind of a waste to just put this grain on the altar and burn it up. Maybe we could give it to the poor instead. Or maybe we could give it to the priests and let it be their salary." Such suggestions have obvious merit, but the problem comes when, over time, people begin to forget the real reason for making these offerings. They begin to think, "God wants me to give up some of my grain

so that the poor can be fed or the priests can be paid." That
had not been the original idea. Such concerns are only
afterthoughts, and even if they are *good* afterthoughts, they
do not represent the real reason for the offerings. The primary purpose of sacrifice is worship (Psalm 54:6; 96:8-9).

I don't know for sure if anything like that ever happened
in ancient Israel, but something similar has happened in
Christian churches. Many people seem to think that the
reason we have an offering during the Sunday morning
service is because the church needs to pay its bills and also
wants to do good things with the money that is collected.
Your church does need to pay its bills, and it probably does
do good things with the money you put in the offering plate
. . . but that is *not* why we have an offering during the Sunday morning service.

The offering is an act of worship, an instance in which
we are invited to give up something that we value — our
money — as a sacrifice to God. In many ways, it is the high
point of the liturgy. We come to church to worship God
and at no other point in the service are we provided with so
pure an opportunity for worship as this.

Think about this for a moment. We sing hymns of
praise to God: "How Great Thou Art," "Praise to the Lord,
the Almighty," "Beautiful Savior." When I sing those
hymns, I do try to take the words to heart and really mean
them as an expression of my devotion and thanksgiving to
the Lord who is so good to me. But words can come easily
and the Bible speaks of people who honor God with their
lips while their hearts are far from God (Isaiah 29:13; Mark
7:6). The connection between hearts and treasures is more

secure: "Where your treasure is, there your heart will be also" (Matthew 6:21). I find that this is true: on a simple, practical level, I find that it is easier to sing hymns and not really mean them than it is to part with my money and not really mean it.

We are invited to put money in the offering plate on Sunday morning not because the church needs our money but because *we want and need to give it.* We have a spiritual need to worship God, and through our offerings we are able to express our love and devotion for God in a way that is simple and sincere. The motivation of the giver is what counts most, not the size of the gift or degree of benefit to the recipient (see Mark 12:42-44).

The good news of stewardship is that church offerings are not fund-raising rituals but acts of worship in which we are invited to express our heartfelt devotion to the God who is so good to us. If we think the point of the offering is collecting funds to meet the church's budgetary expenses then we will probably derive no more satisfaction from this portion of the liturgy than we do from paying our gas bill. Why should it be part of the church service at all? Why not just send out notices in the mail and let church members write checks and mail them in, as they do when tending to other financial commitments? Indeed, many churches now encourage their members to do exactly that — they even set up electronic transfers that allow for donations to be deducted automatically from the parishioners' check-ing accounts. I actually have nothing against this; in fact, I think it's a great way to make sure that members give their intended contributions toward meeting the church's operating expenses. But churches that do this *still* have offerings on Sunday morning. Why? Because the purpose of the Sunday morning offering is not to collect funds for covering the church's operating expenses. The Sunday offering is a worship event that provides us with an opportunity for expressing our love for God in the purest way imaginable, by giving up something that we value.

⚡ Giving as an act of worship takes us beyond duty to delight.

The essence of faith is worship and the essence of worship is sacrifice — giving of ourselves in devotion to God. In that regard, ancient Israelites and modern Christians are the same. There is more to the matter, but this is the first, and possibly the most important thing to learn about biblical stewardship: we give to God as an act of worship.

🎁 *Gifts of Love*

A PENTECOSTAL PASTOR TOLD ME a story about worship. He said that when he was a child he lived in a small town and, on one occasion, his mother sent him to a florist to pick up some flowers for the dinner table. He had to carry the flowers through town from the store to his home and he was embarrassed to do this. He was afraid that his friends would see him and call him a sissy for carrying flowers. But a few years later, he was in love with a young woman and he returned to that same florist's shop, purchased a bouquet for the object of his affection, and car-

🦌 Why God Gives to Us

Giving is a natural expression of love. Friends do it. Lovers do it. Parents do it. Even children do it. We give presents to those we love.

The Bible says that "God gives to all mortals life and breath and all things," so that "in him we live and move and have our being" (Acts 17:25, 28). A psalmist says, "O Lord, how manifold are your works! . . . The earth is full of your creatures. . . . They all look to you to give them their food in due season. . . . When you open your hands, they are filled with good things" (Psalm 104:27-28). Jesus says that the Father in heaven gives "good things to those who ask him" (Matthew 7:11).

The word for this "giving" is *grace*. Jesus gives his life as a ransom for many (Mark 10:45). Eternal life is a gift of God (Romans 6:23). So is the faith necessary to receive it (Ephesians 2:8).

Why does God give these things to us? Because God loves us and there is an intrinsic connection between giving and love. The best known verse of the Bible says, "For God so loved the world that he *gave* . . ." (John 3:16).

God gives because God loves. God gives to *us* because God loves *us*. And when we give our offerings to God as an act of worship we reflect that love. We love God back.

Paul Tournier puts it this way: "There comes a day when we understand that all is of grace, that the whole world is a gift of God, a completely generous gift. We see each flower, each drop of water, each minute of our life as a gift of God. He gives them to all, both to those who know him and to those who are ignorant of him" (*The Meaning of Gifts*, p. 59).

ried it through the same streets without shame. "I was no longer concerned with what anyone would think of me," the pastor concluded. "I was just thinking of her, and of how happy she would be to get flowers, and of how happy I was to be the one to bring them to her."

There is a strong connection between *love* and *giving*. Most of us know what it is like to love someone so much that we want to give them things. The motivation for such gifts is not primarily obligation but desire — we give not because it is something we *should* do but because it is something we *want* to do. Of course, there may be *some* sense of obligation. We are generally expected to get gifts for our loved ones at certain times and on certain occasions regardless of how we feel about it. Still, in a healthy relationship, we do not give only or always out of a sense of obligation. We take a certain excitement in providing gifts for those we love and, sometimes, we may give them things for no reason at all. Such giving is not particularly practical. The point is not what the person needs or whether they will use the gift in a manner that we find acceptable; the point is simply expressing our devotion through an offering of love. The young man in the story above did not stop to ask, "Does she *need* flowers? Maybe school supplies would be more practical." Likewise, giving to the church as an act of worship is not geared specifically to meeting budget needs (as important as those may be). We do have an obligation, a duty to support our church's life and mission, but giving as an act of worship takes us beyond duty to delight.

The Bible is filled with instances of such giving. In the Old Testament, after Noah exits the ark the first thing he does is build an altar and offer sacrifices to God (Genesis 8:20). Later, the patriarch Jacob experiences God's presence in a dream and, not knowing what else to do, sets up a stone and pours oil over the top of it (Genesis 28:16-18). The consistent point seems to be that when people are struck by the goodness of God, they naturally want to give something to God: they don't always know how to do that, but they want to do it. We could ask, "What does God need with dead animals or wasted oil?" but that hardly seems to be the point. These people who had been touched by the goodness of God wanted to worship God, and they did that by taking something that belonged to them and giving it to God in the only way they knew how.

Turning to the New Testament, we see the story of the Magi bringing their gifts to celebrate the birth of the baby Jesus (Matthew 2:1-12). These mysterious visitors from the east travel a great distance for no other purpose than to worship the one who has been born "king of the Jews." When they arrive, they kneel down before him and offer him gifts of gold, frankincense, and myrrh. And then they go home. The Bible says nothing at all about the practical value of these gifts, about what Joseph and Mary do with the gold, much less with the frankincense or the myrrh. The Bible is only interested in telling us that the Magi make such offerings — they give of their treasures in a pure act of worship that expresses their devotion to the newborn Messiah.

When Jesus is grown to adulthood, he receives a similar gift of devotion from a woman who pours expensive ointment on his feet and then wipes his feet with her hair (Mark 14:3-9; see also John 12:1-8). Some people in the story think that this is "a waste," that the woman should have done something more practical with the valuable ointment — maybe sell it and give the money to the poor. But, for Jesus, that is beside the point. The gift is offered as an expression of love and adoration and he says that what the woman has done will always be remembered and told as part of the gospel story.

On a different occasion, Jesus encounters someone who does decide that the best way of showing devotion to God is by helping the poor. Zacchaeus, the rich tax collector, is so inspired by his visit with Jesus that he announces he will give half of his wealth to the poor (Luke 19:1-10). This account makes for an interesting comparison with another story in which Jesus tells a man to sell *all* of his possessions and give the money to the poor (Luke 18:1-25). The man in the latter story is unable to do what Jesus suggests and he goes away sad, disappointing both himself and Jesus. Why would Jesus tell one rich man that he ought to give up all his possessions and then be delighted with another rich man who offers to give up only half? Perhaps the answer is to be found in the person's motivation. The one man wants to know what he *should* do, and Jesus tells him (he should give up all). With Zacchaeus, however, the question of what one *should* do never comes up; he *wants* to give away half his fortune and Jesus is pleased with his heartfelt generosity.

On yet another occasion Jesus meets a widow who out-does Zacchaeus by giving away all that she has — though in this case "all that she has" is only a penny (Mark 12:41-44). Jesus points this woman out to his disciples as an example of profound sacrifice, as someone who out of her poverty gives more than the rich do out of their abundance: everything she has, all she has to live on. It is curious to note, however, that Jesus praises this widow for making a gift to a temple that he has just recently condemned as a corrupt institution. He called the temple a "den of robbers" (Mark 11:17) and specifically faulted the temple leaders for financing their own extravagance with money from widows (Mark 12:40). Why, then, does Jesus praise this widow for giving her money to a cause that he apparently thinks is unworthy of her support? The focus, again, appears to be on the attitude with which she makes the offering. Jesus does not praise the widow's choice of beneficiaries but the sacrificial spirit that moves her to give all she has in devotion to God.

> 🎵 **One of our greatest needs is to worship God.**

The common theme in these stories is that the focus is not on giving as an obligation but on giving as an act of worship. Perhaps the first woman should have sold her ointment and given the money to the poor (as Zacchaeus did). Perhaps Zacchaeus should have given away all of his money (as the widow did). Perhaps the widow should have given her penny to some institution more worthy than the temple that Jesus had condemned. Yet all of these persons are praised by Jesus and presented in the Bible as examples of faithful stewardship. Why? Because they offer their treasures in a spirit of devotion and adoration, as the gifts of glad and generous hearts that have been touched by God's love.

God may be pleased, indeed delighted, with us even if we are giving the wrong amount, even if are giving to unworthy or inappropriate causes. As we learn more about stewardship, of course, we will want to grow in those respects. We can spend a lifetime trying to find better ways of fulfilling God's expectations. But, for starters, our principal concern in giving should not be where to give, or how to give, or how much to give. First, let us focus on the *why*. If we give with hearts that have been touched with God's love, if we give with hearts full of devotion for the God who loves us, then the questions of *where* and *how* and *how much* will work themselves out in time.

🎚 *Giving Thanks*

I ONCE SERVED AS A pastor in a congregation where the people wanted me to visit all of the "inactive members" and see if we could get some of them to come back to church. I came up with a list of fifty families and decided that I would visit one family each week for a year. I guess I wasn't very good at this because I didn't persuade too many people to come back to the church. But I sure did hear some stories.

I heard lots of reasons why people had quit coming to church. Some of the inactive members had complaints about liturgy or about church politics or about personal conflicts within the congregation. Some of them thought the church had gotten too liberal, or that it wasn't contemporary enough, or that the services were boring, or that the programs we offered didn't meet their needs.

I tried to find a common denominator and eventually I

did. All of the people I visited told me in one way or another that they had quit coming to church because they weren't "getting out of it" whatever it was that they thought they should get out of it. People had different ideas with regard to what they thought the church should do for them, but all of the inactive members agreed that, whatever that was, the church had failed to do what they thought it should do for them.

This surprised me because when I was a child and my family went to church on Sunday morning, my mother used to tell us, "We are going to worship God." I'm not sure if it even occurred to me that I was supposed to get anything out of it. Certainly, that wasn't the reason we went. I didn't know very much about church or about what it all meant, but even at a very young age I knew that it wasn't about *me* — at least, it wasn't *all* about me. These people didn't come from all over town Sunday after Sunday just to get together and meet my needs. No. They came to worship God.

"Six days a week God blesses us," my mother would say, "and on Sundays we give thanks." That has always stuck with me, although I know that there is more to it than that. Pastors and worship leaders work very hard to provide their congregations with services that they hope will be meaningful and inspirational to all who come. Of course. But I still think my mother was right: the *main* reason for going to church is not to get our needs met; the main reason, the most important reason, for going to church is to worship God.

And now that I am (a lot) older, I have discovered something else. When people do this — when they come to church to worship God — something wonderful happens.

They invariably discover that they are much more likely to get something out of the experience than if they had come for any other reason. I don't know why this is — maybe God just has a sense of irony. Or maybe the point is that one of our greatest needs *is* to worship God. We don't always know this, but it is true nonetheless, and when we quit focusing on ourselves and focus instead on worshiping the God who is so good to us, one of our deepest needs is met. We just didn't know, perhaps, that *that* was what we needed.

So, worship is essential to faith. But I have also said that *sacrifice* is essential to worship. Why is that? Because worship, almost by definition, is the opposite of self-centeredness. When we worship God, we make God (rather than ourselves) the center of our devotion. Doing this always involves some element of self-denial or sacrifice, giving up something that we value, giving up attention to *our* wants and *our* needs in order to focus on God.

People give money for all sorts of reasons, but the good news of biblical stewardship is that we are encouraged to give out of glad and generous hearts, motivated by sincere love for God. If we give out of a sense of compulsion (motivated by guilt or shame) or out of self-interest (to win praise or gain influence), there is a good chance that we will end up feeling used. We may think that our generosity has not been fully appreciated or we may wonder whether the money we gave has been put to the best possible use. But giving that is grounded in the good news of biblical stewardship never leaves us with those hollow emotions. When we give cheerfully, as an act of worship, the very act of giving moves us to lose interest in ourselves and to devote ourselves to God. We may care about how the money that we give is used but that isn't the *reason* we give it. We may appreciate having our gifts acknowledged, but that isn't *why* we give them. In some mysterious way, such giving — motivated only by our love for God — ends up meeting our *own* deepest spiritual needs and is intensely satisfying. I have never known anyone to give their money in such a way and later regret it.

Indeed, there is something basic about such giving that goes beyond the expectations of any particular religion. In his book *Stewards of God,* Milo Kauffman relates the story of a poor Hindu in Nepal who brought the last of his rice as an offering to his god. A neighbor told him, "You must not do that. You have to live." His answer was, "No. I *don't* have to live. But I do have to worship" (p. 174).

At some level, this man was experiencing the same truth as the widow Jesus met in the temple (Mark 12:41-43). To be perfectly honest, I am a little troubled by both stories because, on a common sense level, I don't know if it is really a good idea for poor men and women to give their last bowls of rice or copper coins (or Social Security checks, for that matter) to religious causes. I think that maybe I would have told the widow to keep her coins and the Hindu man to keep his rice. But, on another level, one that is less invested in "common sense," I do understand the motivation: for those who make the discovery, *worship* is what makes life worthwhile.

Discussion Questions

1. Think about the "offering" collected during services at your church. Do you experience this moment in the liturgy as an act of worship, or does it just seem like an occasion for taking care of business?

2. How have you experienced *giving* as an expression of love in your own life (as either the giver or receiver of gifts)? How might this work in your relationship with God?

3. What is your main motivation for going to church? Has this changed over the years?

4. What would church be like if everyone in the congregation gathered, not to have their own needs met, but simply to praise and worship God? How would such a singular focus on worship affect your home congregation? What would be different — and how would that make you feel?

5. Read again the story of the boy who made two trips to a florist (pages 13-15). What does this have to say about worship?

CHAPTER TWO

An Expression of Faith

*Think of us this way, as servants of Christ and
stewards of God's mercies.*

1 Corinthians 4:1

MY WIFE AND I HAVE four cats. We also own a home and
we have done what we can to keep it up and to furnish it
properly. We have basic electronic equipment and some
decent furniture. We've hung pictures on our walls and ac-
cented the hardwood floors with attractive rugs. We think
it's a nice house, filled with nice things — though I admit
that the furniture and the rugs could probably be a bit
nicer if we didn't have four cats!

We travel almost every year, and when we do, we find
someone to live in our home and take care of both it and
the cats. Usually, this is a student who is happy to get out of
a cramped dorm room. The student cooks in our kitchen,
sleeps in our bed, watches our TV, and just generally pre-
tends that she or he is the owner of a middle-class home
for a few weeks. It's not a bad deal for the non-allergic,
though the litter-box duties can be a tad daunting.

In biblical terms, this student is a *steward*. Stewards are people who live in a place that they do not own, making full use of (but also taking care of) things that do not belong to them. In the Bible, Abraham had a steward, a servant "who had charge of all that he had" (Genesis 24:2). Joseph was a steward of Potiphar in Egypt (Genesis 39:1-6) and, then, later had a steward of his own (Genesis 44:1-5). In the New Testament, stewards (sometimes called "managers") are mentioned in Matthew 20:8, Luke 8:3, and John 2:8. And Jesus tells "stewardship parables" about travelers who go on journeys and leave others in charge of their possessions (Matthew 21:33-43; 24:45-51; 25:14-30; Luke 16:1-10). Typically, these parables provide examples of "good stewards" and "bad stewards." Good stewards are described as "faithful and wise" (Matthew 24:45) or as "good and trustworthy" (Matthew 25:21, 23). Bad stewards are called "wicked and lazy" (Matthew 25:26; 24:48).

So far, all of the students who have cared for our belongings have been good stewards and we have never regretted letting them live in our home and use our belongings. But what if we were to return to find the house trashed, to discover that the person we had allowed into our home had thrown wild parties, broken all the china, soiled the furniture, and just tossed the cats outside to fend for themselves? That would be a bad steward.

One of the first things we might say about stewardship, then, is fairly obvious. We live in this world as stewards of God, entrusted with caring for all that God so generously allows us to use. But we can go deeper. According to the Bible, bad stewardship is not just a matter of negligence or

carelessness. The root cause of bad stewardship is often a
fundamental misunderstanding or false claim regarding
ownership.

Sometimes, stewards forget that they are stewards and
think that the property entrusted to them is actually their
own. In any event, they behave as though it were their own,
as though they were owners rather than merely stewards
of what belongs to someone else. Thus, Jesus talks about
a man who places tenants in charge of his vineyard. When
he sends servants to collect "the fruit of the vineyard,"
the tenants beat and abuse these servants and send them
away empty. They even kill the boss's son in a misguided
attempt to keep control of the vineyard, which they have
apparently decided belongs to them (Matthew 21:28-41).
There are many things wrong with such a scenario, but the
basic problem is that the stewards think they are in charge
when they are not. It is an issue of *ownership.*

What if my wife and I were to return from our travels to
discover our hired student had changed the locks on our
doors and taken up permanent residence in our home?
Suppose we confronted him and he said, "It's all mine
— you *gave* it to me!" "No," we would say. "We were just
allowing you to use what still belongs to us. There was no
transfer of ownership." So, in his stewardship parables, Jesus indicates that a fundamental problem with humans is
that they don't always realize God is only letting them use
what *still belongs to God.*

❧ A High Privilege

THE POSITION OF SCRIPTURE IS that we *are* stewards
— it is not something we choose to be. We may choose to
be faithful stewards or unfaithful stewards, but that we *are*
stewards is a given. Even people who do not realize that
they are stewards are stewards nonetheless.

I know that stating the situation like this has a negative cast that lends itself easily to guilt-inducing rhetoric.
Still, my goal in presenting this teaching is not to make
anyone more aware of his or
her inadequacies. That might
initially be an unavoidable
side effect, but the eventual
goal is to present "living as a
steward" as an attractive call-
ing that we will be able to embrace with confidence and joy.

> ✒ **Even people who do
> not realize that they are
> stewards are stewards
> nonetheless.**

We should at least realize what a high privilege it is to
be stewards of God. The Bible teaches that God has chosen
us to have dominion over all that God has made, to care
for God's creation as majestic beings who are but "a little
lower" than God and the angels (Genesis 1:28; Psalm 8:3-8;
Hebrews 2:5-8). Beyond that, God has entrusted Christians
with the precious gift of the gospel (1 Corinthians 4:1;
2 Corinthians 5:18-20; 1 Peter 4:10). It is through us that
God chooses to continue the gracious act of "reconciling
the world to himself" through Christ (2 Corinthians 5:18-
20). God has appointed us to be the "light of the world"
and the "salt of the earth," the people whose good works
will inspire others to glorify the Father in heaven (Matthew

5:14-16). We are the agents through whom God has chosen
to bring about God's purposes: love and joy and peace.

There is a tendency for such acclamations to produce
immediate shame: we are conscious of all the ways in
which humans have *not* cared for God's creation and in
which Christians have *not* been living testimonies to God's
grace. But let us realize that it is God who names us stewards. We did not apply for the job — God chose us, and, we
must assume that God knew what God was doing. Perhaps
God sees things in us that we do not see in ourselves —
potential that is not always realized.

Theologian Douglas John Hall has explored what is
implied by the symbolism of calling people *stewards.* He
tells us that this "ancient piece of wisdom about the human vocation" locates us in the grand scheme of things:
not divine, but divinely chosen. From one perspective we
may seem mediocre and vulnerable, yet from another, how
wonderful and marvelous we are — "what a piece of work,"
to quote *Hamlet* (Act 2, scene 2, line 303; compare this to
Psalm 139:14). We are not masters of the universe, but we
are not mere robots or puppets of God either. The biblical teaching of stewardship "puts an enormous question
mark over all human presumption" while simultaneously
allowing that we may be more worthy of exaltation than
we are prone to imagine. We own nothing, but manage
everything. God trusts us in a way that we are reluctant to
trust each other (or ourselves) and places confidence in us
beyond anything that our record thus far would seem to
warrant.

Most of us probably know that we have not excelled at

being stewards of all that God has given us; at least, we realize that we could do better. Let us acknowledge this, but try to move on. The biblical teaching about steward-ship is good news, for the recognition that we are *only* stewards and not owners is actually quite liberating — especially when we realize who the real owner is!

Here, then, is a basic principle of biblical stewardship: *everything we are and everything we have belongs to God.* This is an article of faith that Christians of all varieties acknowledge (as do adherents of many other religions). In many liturgical churches, the Sunday offering is presented at the altar with the following prayer:

> We offer with joy and thanksgiving *what you have first given us* — ourselves, our time, and our possessions. . . .

And perhaps the best known stewardship hymn in Chris-tendom paraphrases 1 Chronicles 29:14 to proclaim,

> *We give thee but thine own,*
> *Whate'er the gift may be;*
> *All that we have is thine alone,*
> *A trust, O Lord from thee.*

In a basic sense, stewardship is really just a matter of put-ting such faith into action, figuring out what it means to believe this, in down-to-earth, practical terms, and then living accordingly. Stewardship is an expression of faith that moves from creed to practice, from merely claiming to believe something to living out that belief in real and obvious ways.

I like to say that stewardship puts into practice our faith in God as our Creator, our Redeemer, and our Sustainer.

🐚 *God Our Creator*

THE BIBLE TEACHES THAT EVERYTHING belongs to God for one simple reason: God created everything — including us. Psalm 100:3 says it nicely:

> *Know that the Lord is God*
> *It is he that made us, and we are his.*

So does Psalm 24:1:

> *The earth is the Lord's and all that is in it;*
> *the world, and those who live in it.*

Of course, we might also go to the very first chapters of the Bible, to the poem of creation in Genesis 1 or to the narrative of Adam and Eve in Genesis 2-3.

Christians also connect Jesus Christ with this work of creation. "He was in the beginning with God," the Gospel of John says. "All things came into being through him, and without him not one thing came into being" (John 1:2-3). Likewise, the letter to the Colossians testifies that "in him all things in heaven and on earth were created" and, indeed, that "all things have been created through him and for him" (Colossians 1:16).

The God whom we call "Father, Son, and Holy Spirit" is the Creator of all that we are and all that we have. There are many implications of believing in this Creator. First, everything may be regarded as basically good, for nothing that God makes can be intrinsically bad (Genesis 1:31; 1 Timothy 4:4). Everything in creation has a place in this good world that God has made. And if God is the author of all life, then all *people* are God's children, beloved of God and deserving of God's care. Our own selves — our own *bodies* are as God made them and we are to appreciate their goodness without complaining or asking, "Why have you made me like this?" (Romans 9:20).

Second, human beings have a unique role in God's creation in that they are entrusted with caring for everything else. As the psalmist says, "You have given them dominion over the works of your hands; you have put all things under their feet" (Psalm 8:6). We are responsible to God for protecting, preserving, and, indeed, enjoying all that God has made.

But perhaps the most important implication of believing in God as Creator is, quite simply, believing that *we are creations*. This is only logical, but in my experience, many people find it easier to believe that God is the Creator than to believe that they are creations — that their very existence, their personality, their intellect, and all of their various traits and abilities ultimately derive from something other than themselves.

"What do you have that you did not receive?" Paul asks.

"And if you received it, why do you boast, as if it were not a gift?" (1 Corinthians 4:7). For me, the single most meaningful moment in worship each year comes on Ash Wednesday when my pastor or some other church leader traces the sign of a cross on my forehead and says, "Remember that you are dust, and to dust you shall return" (see Genesis 3:19). Remember! We bring nothing into this world and we will take nothing out of it (Job 1:21). Everything we have, we have because of what we are — and everything we are, we owe to God.

Someone will say, "I went to school and worked hard to learn certain skills. I got a job and now I work long hours, using those skills. For this I receive a paycheck and I should be allowed to use that money in whatever manner I please. It's mine. I earned it." Believing in God as Creator prompts us to think again. I owe my physical body and my mental and emotional health to God. I may have studied hard in school, but God gave me the brains and the capacity to learn. I may work long hours, but God provides me with the strength and stamina to do so. Moses told the Israelites long ago, "Do not say to yourself, 'My power and the might of my own hand have gotten me this wealth.' But remember the Lord your God, for it is he who gives you power to get wealth" (Deuteronomy 8:17-18). So, I might have good reason to be proud of my accomplishments, but this pride must be tempered by knowledge that I am a creation — and a creation is quite literally *nothing* without its Creator.

And as for that paycheck — yes, of course, we should be allowed to use our money in whatever manner we please.

The question is not what we are *allowed* to do with our
money but what we might *want* to do with it. People who
know that they are creations, who truly realize that all they
are and all they have belongs to God, sometimes want to
use their money differently than they would if they did not
realize this.

⚘ *God Our Redeemer*

THE BIBLE TEACHES THAT GOD has redeemed us from
bondage, delivered us from the devil, freed us from sin and
death so that . . . what? So that we might be free agents,
living our lives as sheep without a shepherd? No. God has
redeemed us so that we might belong to God, live in God's
kingdom, thrive and prosper under God's providential
care.

This is a *second* reason why everything we are and everything we have belongs to
God. Theologians will say it
shouldn't even be necessary:
we already belong to God
because of creation. But here
is another reason all the same. St. Paul puts it this way:
"You are not your own, for you were bought with a price"
(1 Corinthians 6:19-20). The "price" to which Paul refers is
the precious blood of our Lord Jesus Christ. Jesus gave his
life as a "ransom" for us (Mark 10:45). We have been saved
from death and hell and, now, the Bible says, we are to live
for the Christ who died for us (2 Corinthians 5:15).

> ♪ **God has redeemed us
> so that we might belong
> to God.**

I think that people sometimes think of this as "the catch." We are glad that Christ has died for us, but we view "living for him" as an obligation rather than as a privilege. We know that the wages of sin are death (Romans 6:23), and we certainly don't want to go to hell, so we are very glad that Jesus was willing to die for our salvation. The catch, to put it crassly, is that we now owe him "big time." It is a debt we can never repay and preachers may become adept at calling our attention to this fact: "Think of what Christ did for you! What have you done for him in return? Is it enough?" Of course, it is never enough. How could it be?

I want to suggest looking at the matter differently. Redemption is "a free gift" (Romans 6:23). Belonging to God and living for Christ are not means by which we seek to repay God for what God has done. Rather, belonging to God and living for Christ are ways of describing what it means to be redeemed. It is not a response to salvation; it *is* salvation. It is part of the gift.

To understand this better, let's go back to one of God's first great acts of redemption, delivering the Israelites from slavery in Egypt (see Exodus 3–14). As you may recall, God brings the children of Israel out of bondage through Moses, who boldly tells Pharaoh, "Let my people go!" There is a dramatic exodus, a stirring escape through the Red Sea, and then . . . they are free. But God does not just leave them there in the middle of the desert or abandon them to their own devices. Rather, God becomes their Lord, ruling them, providing for them, protecting them, and, yes, giving them commandments.

For the Israelites, redemption did not mean having no

god; it meant having a loving and benevolent God. If that had not been an option — if God had simply brought the Israelites out of slavery and then left them, my guess is that they would not have remained free. Some of them may have returned to Pharaoh (Numbers 14:3). Others may have ended up serving some other god or something even worse: a golden calf, perhaps, or maybe just the gold that it was made from, or, quite possibly, the people who *had* the gold (Exodus 32:1-4).

Bob Dylan said, "You're gonna have to serve somebody" and that seems to be true. Absolute freedom in the sense of not ever having to answer to anyone for anything, of not ever needing to rely on anyone for anything, does not appear to be an option in this life. Even if it were an option, it would not be a very good one because, the truth is, God is better at managing our lives than we are!

Of course, we may not always realize this. Sheep do not necessarily want to have shepherds. If it were left up to them, many sheep would probably just as soon go out into the world on their own, footloose and fancy-free. But that is because they are sheep: they do not realize that green pastures and still waters sometimes have to be provided, and they may not give adequate consideration to "the wolf factor."

Even so, the author of the Twenty-Third Psalm has not resigned himself to accepting the Lord as his shepherd because that is "the right thing to do" or because he figures he owes God that much. He is delighted to announce, "The Lord is my shepherd!" because, apparently, he knows that he needs a shepherd and has discovered to his delight that

God is willing to take the job. To realize that God will lead him, protect him, and provide for him, to know that he can belong to God, is an occasion for almost inexpressible joy.

When God told the people of Israel, "I will be your God and you shall be my people" (Leviticus 26:12; Jeremiah 11:4; 30:22), they did not respond by thinking, "Aw, I *knew* there'd be a catch! God saved us — but now we have to be God's people!" No. Being God's people was what redemption was all about. It wasn't payback for salvation; it *was* salvation.

Jesus renewed this proclamation when he strode into Galilee and announced, "The kingdom of God has come near!" (Mark 1:15). Throughout his ministry, Jesus described God's kingdom as something that was *near,* something that people could *seek* (Matthew 6:33), something that they could *enter* (John 3:5), something that was *among* them (Luke 17:21).

> 🔊 **Being God's people was what redemption was all about.**

By speaking of God's kingdom in such terms, Jesus meant to emphasize that people do not have to die and go to heaven to live in a realm of power ruled by God. Already, in this life, Jesus says, God is ready and willing to rule our lives. And this, he adds, is "good news" (Mark 1:14-15).

Believing in God as Redeemer means believing that we have been redeemed. And being redeemed means living freely under the rule of God. God has not just set us free from tyrannical, evil powers but has also pledged to be our lord and rule our lives. Just as "lack of misery" is not the same thing as joy, so "being set free from bondage" is not all there is to redemption. We do not realize how much God offers us until we enter into the kingdom of God and experience what it means to have God rule our lives.

So what does this have to do with stewardship? We observed above that, like it or not, everything we are and everything we have belongs to God because God created all that there is and has never renounced ownership of any of it. Believing in God as Redeemer leads us to see that this is *good news* because those who belong to God benefit from the guidance and protection that God's rule over their lives affords. Think of it this way: if God allowed the blood of Jesus to be shed in order to obtain you, do you not think that God will take pretty good care of you? Those who have been "bought with a price" are precious to God and can be confident of God's wise and benevolent care.

To drive this home in a practical sense, you might consider what it would mean for God to take charge of one specific area of your life. What would happen if God were in charge of your finances? Would you use your money differently? How much money would you have? If God were truly in charge of your finances, do you think that you would have *less* money than you do now? Or do you think that you might have *more* money than you do now?

What would happen if God were in charge of your finances?

I can see those last questions going either way. In the Bible, God sometimes prospers people and increases their wealth — see, for instance, the stories of Abraham (Genesis 24:35), Isaac (Genesis 26:12-16), and Jacob (Genesis 30:43).

🌿 Some Thoughts on God's Gifts to Us

"Every day we stand in the shade of trees we did not plant. We live in houses we did not build. We eat food we did not produce. We ponder ideas that are not original to us. So, too, we live in a body and with a mind and a spirit that we did not choose or create."

Donald W. Hinze, To Give and Give Again: A Christian Imperative for Generosity, *pp. 89-90.*

"All the difference in the world exists between those who recognize and willingly accept their stewardship, realizing the gracious and bountiful and loving gifts of God, and those who set out with the attitude of putting a fence around as much of the universe as possible and saying, This is mine. It isn't. And nothing we do can make it so."

Turner N. Clinard, Responding to God: The Life of Stewardship, *p. 14.*

But, in other cases, people are told to sell their possessions and give their money away (Mark 10:21). I have no way of knowing what God might do in your case, but I think I can promise you this: if you put God in charge of your finances, your life will be better, not worse. When we put God in charge of *any* area of our lives, our lives get better, not worse.

🌾 God Our Sustainer

THE BIBLE TEACHES THAT GOD sustains us in our weakness, and strengthens us when we are weary. "They who wait for the Lord shall renew their strength," the prophet Isaiah promises (Isaiah 40:31). "I can do all things through him who strengthens me," the apostle Paul testifies (Philippians 4:13).

Christians experience this sustaining power of God in a variety of ways. The Bible says that when we come to God in prayer and thanksgiving, "the peace of God, which surpasses all understanding," guards our hearts and minds in Christ Jesus (Philippians 4:6-7). It tells us that Jesus remains present with us always (Matthew 28:20) and that we experience this presence when we come together with others in his name (Matthew 18:20). It says that the Holy Spirit comes as a Helper or Advocate to those who need God's counsel or care (John 14:25).

Faith in God as our Sustainer translates into a single word: *trust.* "Do not worry about anything," Paul advises. "My God will fully satisfy every need of yours according to his riches in glory in Christ Jesus" (Philippians 4:6, 19). And Jesus himself says, "Do not let your hearts be troubled, and do not let them be afraid" (John 14:27).

People today experience anxiety over lots of things, but finances are often near the top of the list. This was true in Jesus' day as well. You may remember what he said: "Look at the birds of the air; they neither sow nor reap nor gather into barns, and yet your heavenly Father feeds them. Are you not of more value than they?" (Matthew 6:26). There is no need to worry, Jesus says, about "your life" or about "what you will eat" or "what you will drink" or "what you will wear" (Matthew 6:25). There is more to life than such material concerns, and if we seek God's rule and righteousness, we will discover that all the things we need will be given to us as well (Matthew 6:33).

Jesus does not mean that we should be naive about life. Simply "trusting God to provide" is not presented as a substitute for careful planning, reasonable preparation, or dedicated labor. But there is a basic sense in which recognizing we have a God who loves and provides for us can set us free from the anxieties that would make us "slaves of mammon," to use Jesus' colorful expression (Matthew 6:24).

Near the end of his life, the apostle Paul said, "I know what it is to have little, and I know what it is to have plenty. In any and all circumstances, I have learned the secret. . . ."

What secret? Paul is referring to something that every human being I have ever met would like to know. It is a secret that Paul says sustained him through life when he was well-fed — and when he was hungry; when he was prosperous — and when he was in need.

Here it is: "I have learned to be content with whatever I have" (Philippians 4:11-12).

This sounds so simple, and yet it can be so difficult. And I'm not sure which is harder — being content when one has little or being content when one has plenty. Both are hard; in fact, both may be impossible apart from the secret Paul knew. What he knew was that God was in charge. He knew that everything he had belonged to God. He knew that he himself belonged to God, that he was precious to God, and that the God who valued him so dearly was in charge of his life. And he knew that God would provide for him and sustain him, sometimes with little, sometimes with plenty, but always with

> 🎵 **"I have learned to be content with whatever I have."**

whatever was the right amount for him to have the life God
wanted him to have.

Paul is not alone. Those who know and practice the
good news that the Bible teaches about stewardship invariably come to experience the reality of this secret in their
lives. They become people who trust God to provide them
with what they need to be content and they become people
who *are* content with whatever it is that God provides.
When they have little, they are not envious of those who
have more, and when they have plenty, they are not driven
by an obsession to obtain still more.

Believing in God as Sustainer means believing that
we are sustained — that we have a God who strengthens
us and provides for us and that we can trust this God to
take good care of us. The implications of this belief for
stewardship are simple but obvious: we are free to use our
resources (our time, our talents, and our treasures) in ways
that are pleasing to God without worrying about our own
needs. We offer to God what God has first given us and we
know that God will continue to provide for us and to teach
us the secret of being content.

✵ Conclusion

T. A. KANTONEN SAYS THAT A pastor once told him he
always "blushed when following a sermon he had to announce an offering and thus divert the attention of his
people from the gospel to material things" (*A Theology for
Christian Stewardship*, p. 32). Clearly, this pastor had not

paid attention in seminary, for he did not seem to know what "the gospel" is. The good news revealed to us in Jesus Christ is not some ephemeral message about life in another world — it is a message with clear and direct relevance for the material world in which we now live. The distinguishing mark of the early church, after Pentecost, was the relationship of believers with their possessions (Acts 2:44-45; 4:32-37). For many, the good news or gospel of Jesus Christ meant that there would no longer be a needy person among them. We might not follow the specific example of this church by holding all things in common, but certainly the faith that we proclaim is good news for bodies as well as for souls, good news that touches our daily lives and helps us not only with "religious matters" (whatever those are) but also with fundamental, very material and mundane concerns.

In his first letter to the Corinthians, the apostle Paul moves without any embarrassment from a lofty treatise on the resurrection of Christ to an announcement of an offering that he is collecting (1 Corinthians 15:1–16:4). There is no disconnect between Easter faith and practical living, between praising God for giving us victory over death and giving our money away on a regular basis. Indeed, for Paul, it is because of our Easter faith that we can turn our attention to others and know our labor in the Lord will not be in vain (1 Corinthians 15:58).

Being faithful in stewardship means putting our faith into action. We believe that all we are and all we have belongs to God and we believe that this is good news. Stewardship is about discovering the practical value of our faith. The creeds and confessions that we recite are not just words and talk; they are prescriptions for experiencing life at its best.

Being a faithful steward does not necessarily mean being a person who is a major donor to churches or charities, or being a person who is reluctant to spend money on his or her own pleasures or concerns. Rather, a faithful steward is a person who a) views this world as God's good creation and is grateful to be a part of it; b) knows that God cares for those whom God has made and is ready and willing to rule their lives; and c) trusts God to provide him or her with whatever is needed to be content. Faithful stewardship is a matter of becoming such a person and acting accordingly. Indeed, when faithful stewards do become people who are extraordinarily generous or thrifty, it is because they are living the way that they *want* to live, acting on a faith that tells them they belong to God.

The good news of biblical stewardship is that those who live as people who belong to God experience life at its absolute best. Milo Kauffman says in his book *Stewards of God,* "Joyful people will be generous people, and generous people will be joyful people — it is difficult to say which is cause and which is effect, for either appears to produce the other" (p. 67). It certainly works both ways in the Bible: generosity leads to rejoicing (1 Chronicles 29:9) and joy leads people to give generously (2 Corinthians 8:2). It could become a wondrous cycle, a carousel of cheer and altruism. Who would not want to take a few turns on so marvelous a ride?

Discussion Questions

1. Do you regard your place in this world as one of *stewardship* or *ownership* (see pages 26-27)? What difference does that distinction make with regard to attitudes and actions in life?

2. Why is it "a high privilege" to be called stewards of God? Does God see something in you that you might not see in yourself (pages 28-29)?

3. How would you personally answer the questions posed on page 38: What would happen if God were in charge of your finances? Would you use your money differently? Do you think that you would have less money? Or more?

4. Think about the secret Paul knew: "to be content with whatever I have." Do you know people who have experienced this in their lives? What about you — have you discovered this secret yet, or can you imagine ever becoming a person for whom this is really true?

5. What does it mean to be "a faithful steward"? Read again the paragraph with "a-b-c points" on page 44: Do these points describe the sort of person that you would like to be? Do you think that you can be this person?

CHAPTER THREE

A Spiritual Discipline

"Where your treasure is, there your heart will be also."
Matthew 6:21

SAMUEL CLEMENS — BETTER KNOWN to many as Mark Twain — is said to have been a man who always enjoyed a good argument. One time, so the story goes, he found himself on a train with a Mormon who, in keeping with the teaching of some Mormons at that time, believed in the practice of polygamy. Before long, Clemens and his companion were engaged in a theological dispute over that subject. The Mormon insisted, "There is nothing in the Bible that says a man cannot have more than one wife." Clemens responded, "I may not be too well-read in the scriptures — but I seem to recall something in there that says 'No man can serve two masters.'"

The passage to which he was referring was a verse from the Sermon on the Mount in which Jesus is not actually commenting on domestic relations but on the impossibility of any person, male or female, serving both God and "mammon" (Matthew 6:24). The word *mammon* (sometimes translated "wealth") refers to material things, to money and the things that money can buy. We ought to *use* such things, Jesus implies, not *serve* them.

Like most biblical teachings on stewardship, this is good news. We can be free from that spiral of consumerism that allows financial concerns to rule our lives. And what is true of mammon is true of other types of "treasures" as well — our time, our relationships, whatever we value in this life.

❦ Hearts and Treasures

LET US LOOK NOW AT another saying of Jesus, also from the Sermon on the Mount: "Where your treasure is, there your heart will be also" (Matthew 6:21). This, too, is good news, though it may take a moment to realize why.

First, it can be bad news. I sometimes hear people say that all God really wants is for us to have the right *attitude* toward our money. According to this theory, it does not matter whether we have a lot of money or only a little money, so long as we are careful not to *trust* in our mammon, not to *love* our money, not to be *devoted* to material things. The point of many stewardship sermons then becomes, "Even if you have a lot of treasure, make sure your heart is set on God. Be careful that your heart is with God, not with your treasure."

Well, here's some bad news: If I understand Jesus correctly when he says, "where your treasure is, there your heart will be also," he is telling us that such good intentions are doomed to fail. He is not warning us about what could happen if we are not careful; he is stating flat-out what *will* happen, whether we are careful or not. Where your treasure is, there your heart will be! You can't avoid it. You can't prevent it. Your heart will follow your treasure. That, I grant, may be bad news.

But, on the other hand, Jesus is also prescribing what we can do about this problem, and his prescription holds good news for all who desire a deeper, more spiritual life.

Jesus says, "Where your treasure is, there your heart will be also." A few years ago, I was asked to preach a sermon on this text. I did some work on the sermon and took a break for lunch. As I sat in the drive-through line at Taco Bell, a song by Bonnie Raitt came on the radio. It was a sad song, an expression of unrequited love called "I Can't Make You Love Me." One mournful line from the chorus stood out, a line that featured brokenhearted Bonnie wailing, "You can't make your heart feel something it won't." That's got to be one of the saddest things I've ever heard.

♫ Where your treasure is, there your heart will be!

You can't make your heart feel something it won't. How many people have found that to be true? Have you ever felt like you *should* love someone or something more than you do? But, if you *don't,* what can you do about it? You can't control your heart, can you? You can't *make* yourself love something (or someone) when you don't. Can you?

The thing is, while I was listening to this song, I was also thinking about what Jesus said in the Sermon on the

Mount, and the lines kept getting switched up together in my mind like this:

> *Where your treasure is, there your heart will be also.*
> *You can't make your heart feel something it won't.*
> *Where your treasure is, there your heart will be also.*

And I couldn't help but notice that Jesus is a lot more hopeful on the subject of hearts than Bonnie Raitt (or pretty much anyone else on Top 40 radio). Of course, I know they're talking about completely different subjects — Jesus was not trying to give romantic advice to candidates for the lonely hearts club. I know that. But let's file this away for a moment and come back to it later.

❧ *Loving God*

ONE OF THE SIMPLEST QUESTIONS I ever got as a pastor almost threw me for a loop. I was fresh out of seminary, serving my first year at a parish down in Texas . . . and a woman in the church asked me, "How can I love God more?"

This seemed like something a pastor should be able to answer, but, believe it or not, they'd never taught us this at seminary. All I knew was that people *should* love God with all their heart and soul and mind. And their neighbors as themselves.

Like most pastors, I was pretty good at telling people what they should do. They should love God, they should love one another, they should even love their enemies. They should also care about their church and be committed to God's work in the world. But now, this woman said that she knew this and that it was what she wanted to do. She just didn't know *how*. How do you make your heart love the Lord more than it does? You can't just wish for it to be true and make it so. Of course, you can pray, I told her, but she'd already thought of that. Anything else?

The answer, I think, lies in what are sometimes called *spiritual disciplines.* Christian churches of all denominations teach that there are certain practices that we can do regularly to maintain our spiritual health. Praying before a meal is a common discipline. So is attending church on Sunday mornings. All churches recognize the validity of spiritual disciplines, though they may differ somewhat on which ones they endorse. Some churches encourage meditation; some suggest fasting; some advocate going to private confession. There are groups that favor particular types of prayer, such as using a rosary or speaking in tongues. When it comes to spiritual disciplines, there is a lot of variety among different sects and denominations, but also a good deal of overlap. Almost all churches would recommend that their members practice some routine of Bible reading or of personal or family devotions.

In this book, we have already talked about stewardship as an act of worship and about stewardship as an expression of faith. But the Bible also presents stewardship as a spiritual discipline, and recognition of what it says in this regard is central to an understanding of biblical stewardship as "good news." When we come to understand stewardship as a spiritual discipline we move quickly away from a focus on requirements ("what we are supposed to do") to a discovery of possibilities that we might not have known were available.

Furthermore, of all the spiritual disciplines that are presented in the Bible (and in the teachings of various churches), stewardship is special in that it is the most directly connected to the status and condition of our hearts. This is significant, for religion that does not come "from the heart" is rejected in the Bible as mere "human doctrine" (Mark 7:6-7). Even a cursory reading of Scripture indicates how important it is that our hearts be right with God and set on God. "The Lord does not see as mortals see," the Bible says. "Mortals look on the outward appearance, but the Lord looks on the heart" (1 Samuel 16:7). And as Christians, we all want to be "pure in heart" (Matthew 5:8). But how do we get there? How do we change *within?*

"Where your treasure is, there your heart will be also," Jesus says. I have noticed over the years that seminary students and pastors often get this backwards. I recall one sermon in which the preacher asked us to consider this text. What it means, he said, is that we can tell what people *really* care about by how they spend their money. People put their treasures (their money) where their hearts are. How much do you spend on entertainment? the preacher asked us. How much do you spend on your family? How much do you give to the church? This reveals what your true values are.

I think he had it backwards. He was thinking, "Where your *heart* is, there your *treasure* will be." But Jesus said

---

🌿 Generosity

"Generosity with gifts is the way to spiritual maturity. Sacred and secular history and literature are replete with examples of the crippling effects of gifts hoarded and unshared. People are not naturally disposed to giving, yet, the life we all prize, filled with joy and spiritual depth, is closely tied to giving generously and with thankful hearts."

Donald W. Hinze, To Give and Give Again: A Christian Imperative for Generosity, *p. ix.*

---

it the other way around: "where you put your treasure — that's where your heart will end up." The point isn't that how we spend our money *reveals* what sort of people we *are,* but that how we spend our money *determines* what sort of people we *become.*

Let's remember that "treasure" is not necessarily "money." Our treasure is whatever we value — our money in many cases, but also our time and our possessions and our families and our physical bodies. Whatever we value — that is our treasure. And Jesus says that what we do with our treasures affects our hearts — it determines who we are inside. It determines what sort of people we become.

> 🎵 **How we spend our money determines what sort of people we become.**

This may sound scary, but it is actually very good news! What it means, in essence, is that the sad song isn't true. We *can* make our hearts feel what they don't. We can control our hearts, direct them in ways we want them to go. We

can do so in a very practical way, by deciding what sort of
people we want to be, and then giving our treasure — our
time, our talents, and our money — to those things that we
want to care about.

Jesus was not a fund-raiser. He talked about money a
lot, but not because he wanted people to give to any particular cause. He talked about money because he cared about
us and because he knew that what we do with our money
affects who we are spiritually.

The Bible is filled with stories to illustrate this: Jesus
telling a rich man to give his money to the poor (Mark
10:17-22); Jesus telling a parable about a rich fool who
keeps building bigger barns to hold all his possessions
(Luke 12:16-21); Jesus prompting wealthy Zacchaeus to
become a generous benefactor (Luke 19:1-10). If we don't
read carefully, we may get the impression that Jesus simply
has it in for rich people. But that's not right at all. In every
one of these stories, Jesus obviously cares *for* the rich; he
is concerned about the quality of their lives and, specifically, about the condition of their hearts. Jesus knows that
what such people do with the things that they treasure
determines the condition of their hearts and, indeed, determines what sort of people they will ultimately become.
This principle, furthermore, would apply to the poor as
well as to the rich: the widow who gives a penny has
devoted her heart to God just as surely as the chief tax
collector who donated half his fortune (Mark 2:41-44;
Luke 19:8-9).

🐌 *Proactive Giving*

THE BIBLE SAYS THAT GOD loves a cheerful giver (2 Corinthians 9:7). This means, of course, that we ought not
give reluctantly or because we think we have to, but willingly, because we truly want to. What it does *not* mean is that
stewardship should always be tied to feelings. A philosophy
that connects "sincere giving" with "what feels right" has
no power to carry us through the hard times or to get us out
of slumps; it has no power to facilitate spiritual growth.

Most people know that spiritually healthy people are
good stewards. They are aware, at some level, of the connection between spiritual health and faithful stewardship,
but they assume this is because the former leads to the latter. The good news taught by Jesus is that it can also work
the other way around.

The biblical idea is for giving to be proactive, not reac-
tive (to use modern "buzz words" that, I grant, are never
found in the Bible). Stewardship can be sincere without
being spontaneous, and there is a world of difference between giving *willingly* and simply giving "on a whim."

"Give from the heart!" people say. But Jesus seemed to
speak of something else: Give where you want your heart
to be, and let your heart catch up. Don't just give to things
you care about. Give to things you *want* to care about. Don't
decide the amount of your giving by how much you care,
but by how much you *want* to care. Ask yourself, If I were
the sort of person I would really like to be, *then* what would
I do? How would I spend my money (and my time, and everything else)? Then, do what you would do if you were that

sort of person. Put your treasure where you want your heart to be, and, Jesus promises, your heart will go there.

A time-honored bit of evangelical counsel holds that it is sometimes easier to *act* oneself into a new way of thinking than to *think* oneself into a new way of acting. We can control what happens to our hearts. Whether we are excited or depressed, full of life or dispirited, we can direct our hearts where we want them to go and determine that we will become the sort of people we want to be.

> 🎵 **If I were the sort of person I would really like to be, *then* what would I do?**

What I am suggesting is that there is a direct connection between stewardship and spirituality. This is true even though *spirituality* is a popular topic these days and *stewardship* is not. You can go to almost any bookstore and find numerous works that tell people how to become more spiritual. Apparently there are a lot of people in our world, and in our churches, who would like to be more spiritual. Many of the books on this subject are quite good, but sometimes they advocate quick-fix approaches to spirituality that ignore the basics.

I suppose it is like dieting. When I hear that someone has gone on the "All-Mango Diet," where you eat nothing but mangoes for two weeks . . . well, I try to be open-minded . . . but I want to ask, "What about the basics? Do you ever get any exercise?"

Likewise, I have talked with a few people who seem to be searching for some gimmick that will make them more spiritual without attending to the basics. I talked with a woman who had bought lots of crystals and hung them in her windows because, she said, they would capture spiritual energy and beam it into her house. She said that she was a Christian, so I asked, "Do you ever read the Bible?" No. "Do you pray?" Not much. "Go to church?" Well, no.

Now, I think crystals are pretty. But for Christians, at least, the basic disciplines for becoming a more spiritual person usually involve Bible reading, prayer, and regular worship. It is frankly difficult to imagine anyone growing spiritually without some attention to those three things. And now I am suggesting that there is a fourth: sacrifice. We grow spiritually through renunciation of things that we value. We give of our treasure and our hearts are affected.

The Bible promises that giving — especially *financial* giving — will be rewarded by God. Paul says, "The one who sows bountifully will also reap bountifully . . . you will be enriched in every way for your great generosity" (2 Corinthians 9:6, 11). Such rewards need not be tangible; they may be spiritual — I think that they usually are. Those who give of their earthly treasure experience the spiritual reward of hearts increasingly drawn into the wondrous love of God.

The Spiritual Principle of Renunciation

NOW I'M GOING TO TELL an embarrassing story . . . one that I swore I would never put in print (but here it is). When I was a young college student I loved Jesus dearly and desired nothing more than to be close to him. One evening, I attended a meeting at a Christian coffee house where a visiting evangelist was speaking about the spiritual life. "If you really want Jesus to be first in your life," he said, "then you need to get rid of whatever is second." What did that mean? He continued, "Ask yourself what it is that you love more than anything else. Whatever it is, it will compete for your devotion to Christ. So, eliminate the competition. Get rid of it."

I do not really think that this was good advice. Today, I would have problems with what the evangelist said, both logically and theologically. But such intellectual concerns did not occur to me at the time. As I walked back to my dorm room, I simply asked myself, "What do I love?" It is a good thing I did not have a girlfriend at the time; I doubt that she would have understood my reasons for "getting rid of her"!

The only thing I could think of that I *really* loved was my record collection. It was a pretty impressive one for the time. So when I got back to my dorm, I proceeded to take all of my records and give them away. I just walked up and down the halls handing them to people and I set many of them out on a table for anyone to grab. Word of this spread fast and in half an hour they were all gone. I already had a bit of a reputation for being a religious nut (a "Jesus freak"), and so I imagine that most of the other students thought that I had decided the records were evil — "devil music" or something like that. But that wasn't it at all. I loved those records and I didn't think there was anything wrong with them. They were a constant source of joy and gladness. I gave them away for one reason only: I treasured them and something deep within had moved me to make a sacrifice, to want to give up something I treasured.

As an adult theologian, I can evaluate this incident in my young life and identify problems with the sort of religion that leads one to do things like that. Encouraging renunciation for its own sake may lead some people to make naïve sacrifices they can ill afford or it may encourage them to become overly pleased with themselves or, indeed, to pass judgment upon others who have not made similar commitments (cf. Luke 18:9-14). Worse, it can lead to the suggestion that our relationship with Christ is somehow maintained through our own acts of commitment to him rather than through his commitment to us. One might also ask, if I had really wanted to do something worthwhile, why didn't I give my records to some underprivileged youth instead of just passing them on to people who probably already had more records than they needed? Or why not sell them and give the money to the poor? Good ideas. I just didn't think of any of that. But, nevertheless, today, I remember this somewhat silly act as a sincere expression of struggling faith, of devotion to a Lord I hardly knew and seldom understood. And three decades later, the spiritual benefits are still with me.

Over the years, I have heard dozens of more respectable stories from people who have been moved by their love for Christ to give up something they loved. I remember a couple who had saved money for a cruise and then decided to cancel the trip and use the money to repair a van for a team of traveling missionaries. I know someone who decided (at the store) that she would forgo the large-screen TV she'd

selected and give the money to a seminary scholarship.
And my heart was touched when my own son called from
college one year to say that he wanted us to donate whatever money we would have spent on his Christmas presents
to a world hunger organization.

All of these stories have one thing in common: no one I
have met who has made such a sacrifice has ever regretted
it. Everyone always says the same thing: giving up something I valued *did* something to me — it transformed me,
it affected me, it helped me to become the sort of person I
wanted to be. And, for what it's worth, I can testify to this
myself. It would be easy for me to dismiss the great record
giveaway as an uninformed surge of adolescent piety but
I have never regretted it. I gave up something I loved as an
act of devotion for Christ and it bonded my heart to him
and helped me love him more.

The spiritual principle of *renunciation* is taught in the
Bible and it was consistently taught in the early church.
We don't hear much about it anymore today. Why not? I
suspect the reason is that there have been too many hucksters and con artists over the years who have exploited this
principle for their own greedy purposes. The Bible does
promise spiritual rewards to persons who give away their
treasures, but in recent years it has been easy to turn on the
television and hear these biblical promises being used as
gimmicks for fund-raising. "Give to my ministry," the TV
preacher will say, "and God will reward you with all sorts of
blessings." You may be healed of your diseases. You may
see your prayers answered. You may even receive *material*
blessings. According to such huckster-preachers, God is

not really asking you to give anything away but is merely suggesting a strategy for wise investment.

Responsible preachers and churches want to avoid being associated with these tactics and so they avoid the subject of "spiritual rewards" altogether. But this, too, is unfortunate, because the promises *are* scriptural. Jesus says, "Give . . . and it will be given unto you, a good measure, shaken together, running over" (Luke 6:38). And, again, he says that anyone who has left houses or fields or anything at all for his sake will receive back "a hundredfold" (Matthew 19:29).

Such promises are meant to be taken metaphorically, not as advocating some crass strategy for manipulating God, but they *are* promises and they *are* real. The point that the Bible consistently makes is that "it is more blessed to give than to receive" (Acts 20:35), that renunciation of what one treasures can have consequences that enhance the quality of one's life.

> ✍ **People who renounce their treasure as a spiritual sacrifice to God discover that they are transformed within.**

It doesn't matter whether we are talking about the widow with her penny or Zacchaeus giving away half his fortune: people who renounce their treasure as a spiritual sacrifice to God discover that they are transformed within, drawn closer to God in a manner that helps them to become more spiritual people. Simply put: stewardship is the biblical path to spirituality.

"I want to love God with all my heart," a woman in my church told me.

*"You can't make your heart feel what it won't," our popular
culture insists.*

*"Oh yes, you can," Jesus responds. "Where your treasure is,
there your heart will be also."*

Discussion Questions

1. Are there any "spiritual disciplines" (page 51) that you have found to be meaningful in helping you to maintain your spiritual health? What disciplines are encouraged by your church or by people you know? Are there any new ones that you might like to try?

2. Is it helpful to think of financial giving as a "spiritual discipline"? How is it similar to, or different from, other disciplines you may have practiced?

3. Consider the statement that "how we spend our money determines what sort of people we become" (page 53). Does this sound threatening or promising (or both)? Do you think that it is true?

4. Reflect on the connection between *spirituality* and *stewardship* (page 56). Would you like to be a more spiritual person — and is there anything that you might do with your money that would move you further along that path?

5. What do you make of the author's personal story about giving away his record collection? Have you ever felt moved to do something out of love for God that others might not understand? How do you feel now about what you did?

PART TWO

Our Duty and Delight

They were pleased to do this, and indeed they owe it to them.

Romans 15:27

WE HAVE DISCUSSED THE BIBLICAL concept of stewardship in general and discovered that what the Bible says
about this subject is good news. The Bible presents God as
the creator and supplier of all that we are and of all that we
have. The Bible promises that God will provide for us and,
indeed, rule our lives, directing and enabling us to manage
our affairs more faithfully than we could on our own. The
Bible further assures us that when we offer ourselves and
what we have to God in worship and in faith, we will discover the blessings of a rich spiritual life. In such ways, we
discover the truth of what Jesus said, that it truly is "more
blessed to give than to receive" (Acts 20:35).

We have been talking about finances all along but now
we are going to deal even more deliberately with matters of
money. We are going to discuss how we as Christians are to
use our money for God and we are going to consider what
"giving to God" means in that context.

Let us begin by noting honestly the awkwardness of
the topic. Many ministers and church leaders feel that
financial stewardship is a difficult subject to address, and
I am no exception. For one thing, I do not regard myself
as any sort of role model in this area. I do not think that I
have been exceptionally faithful in stewardship of my own
finances and, though I think I understand what the scriptures teach about the subject, I acknowledge that it is often
easier to talk (or write) about biblical expectations than
to fulfill them. I suspect that this is a common concern
for many ministers and church leaders. Most of us really
do want to practice what we preach and we feel hypocriti-
cal talking to others about matters that we have not mas-

tered ourselves. But that is what we need to do sometimes: preach what we know to be true, preach it to others *and to ourselves,* and keep on preaching it until it takes hold.

I have alluded previously to a second reason why many pastors are reluctant to talk about money. Religious appeals for financial giving have become tainted in our current society as a result of hucksters and con artists who have abused biblical principles for personal gain. One pastor tells me, "When I talk to my congregation about increasing their giving, I get the impression that they think I am asking for a raise." Of course that isn't the case. The real concern is for the spiritual health of the congregation, but in this era of millionaire television evangelists, many people have become wary of preachers asking for money. This pastor continues, "I am concerned about what will happen to this church if it cannot pay its bills, and I'm also concerned about the spiritual condition of members who are not giving as they ought. But whenever I talk about money, people just look at me as though I'm greedy, as if I want to get their money for *myself.*"

A third reason that discussion of finances is an awkward topic is that most of us consider this to be a private matter. For many, there are few things that would fall more solidly under the heading *None of Your Business* than "How I Spend My Money." Accordingly, the church's interest in our personal finances may strike us as invasive — and this only gets worse when the church begins to think of stewardship as more than just fund-raising. It is one thing for the church to ask for contributions to its ministry and quite another for the church to begin telling us what to do with the *rest* of our money! Yet, as we shall see, there is no way for the church to be faithful to the Bible and not do this. Jesus made clear to everyone who followed him that he intended to meddle with their money. He had a lot to say about the subject and very little, if any, of it had to do with asking for donations to his own ministry. So, too, the church over which Jesus Christ is Lord will not limit its interest in our finances to seeking donations to sustain its own programs. There is a lot more to financial stewardship than that and, yes, it does get meddlesome.

Finally, I think that financial stewardship is an awkward topic because our culture has a paradoxical attitude toward wealth. On the one hand, popular culture tends to portray the rich as greedy and unhappy: consider the characterization of Ebenezer Scrooge in *A Christmas Carol* or of Mr. Burns on *The Simpsons.* On the other hand, popular culture shamelessly acknowledges that most people want to be rich: note the success of television shows like *Who Wants to Be a Millionaire?* and even *Who Wants to Marry a Millionaire?* This is nothing new. As a teenager I was certain that the Beatles were right when they sang, "Money can't buy me love," but I could still identify with Tevye from *Fiddler on the Roof* in fantasizing about how grand life would be "if I were a rich man." It is a contradiction, a paradox: most of us know that having money does not guarantee happiness and yet we think that *our* lives would be better, more fulfilling and more satisfying, if only *we* had more money. We all seem to think that we would be exceptions to the rule. We think that even though money does not usually buy happiness, it might in our case.

For such reasons as these, we may be a bit uncomfort-
able moving from a theoretical discussion of what stewardship means to application of stewardship principles in our
personal lives. Still, it is a necessary step if the good news
of what the Bible promises is to bear fruit. I once heard
someone ask, "Why is the church so interested in money?"
Someone else replied, "Maybe it is because *we* are so interested in money!" I think that's it. Our daily lives are very
much concerned with finances: earning money, investing
money, saving money, and spending money. Faith that is
relevant for our daily lives must be concerned with these
things as well.

I am going to divide this section of the book into four
chapters, but the content is perhaps best understood with
reference to certain distinctions that I like to make.

The first distinction is between faithful *living* and
faithful *giving*. God's interest in our money extends beyond what we give to the church (or to charities and other
causes). God is interested in all of our money — how we
make it, what we do with it, and even how we feel about it.
So, in Chapter Four, we will begin with the big picture, accepting the Bible's invitation to faithful living in all matters
related to finances.

The next three chapters all deal with the topic of faithful
giving, which I present as one of the most important ways
in which we can use our money for God. In Chapter Five, I
will provide an overview of what the Bible says about this
aspect of our faithfulness to the gospel of Christ, offering a
vision of the sort of people we can be when the goodness of
God takes hold of our lives.

Chapter Six has a more practical focus and lays out a distinction that I like to make between two different types of giving: *support* and *sacrifice.* As responsible church members, we want to support the church of which we are a part so that it can meet its budget and cover its operating expenses. This is mundane, but very important: churches need to pay their bills and church members must provide the funds for them to do so. But, beyond that, we are also invited to renounce our material possessions by making cheerful sacrifices that take us into a spiritual realm where the real joy of giving abounds. The practical implications of this distinction will become apparent when I lay out a program for giving to the church (or to other charities) that will probably be different from anything you have heard before but that, I think, is biblical, sensible, and eminently doable. Basically, I draw upon the time-honored practices of *pledges* and *offerings,* but I re-interpret these in a way that I believe makes better sense of biblical principles and also respects some pragmatic considerations for life in our modern world. My hope is to provide an approach to giving that encourages faithfulness, helps us to understand *why* we are giving, and helps us to determine just *how much* we want to give. This last point, of course, is the most pragmatic concern of all and, so, we shall devote all of Chapter Seven to a consideration of that simple question: *How much?*

All of these chapters are informed by another distinction, one that we have mentioned previously. Theologians often speak of interpreting Scripture in terms of law and gospel. T. A. Kantonen, for instance, taught that when

people give to the church in order to fulfill obligations of
church membership or to be obedient to their church's
teaching, they are responding to the *law*. When they give
out of gratitude for God's undeserved grace, out of a joyous
and spontaneous willingness to sacrifice, they are responding to the *gospel*. Kantonen clearly thought the latter type
of giving was better and he was probably right. But I don't
think we need to choose between them: it is not a matter
of law *or* gospel but, rather, law *and* gospel. So, in this last
half of the book we will continue to emphasize the good
news of biblical stewardship while also speaking now and
then of obligations and responsibilities. Giving to God can
be our response to both law and gospel and as such it can
become both our duty and our delight.

Discussion Questions

1. Do you find it awkward to talk about money in church or in other social settings? Why do you think that is?

2. How does your church address issues related to money and the Christian life? What do you find helpful? What do you wish could be done differently?

3. What do you hope to get out of the next four chapters of this book? How would you complete the following sentences?

I would be disappointed if these chapters . . .

I would be delighted if these chapters . . .

CHAPTER FOUR

Faithful Living

It is required of stewards that they be found trust-worthy.

1 Corinthians 4:2

THE BIBLE TEACHES THAT EVERYTHING that we think we own actually belongs to God. And Jesus says that we need to give it all to God. At first, this sounds unrealistic, if not impossible, but obviously such a commitment is not to be fulfilled in a literalistic or legalistic sense. Jesus does not expect all of his followers to divest themselves of everything they own and become paupers. The Christian church has always recognized this: although God may call the occasional saint to a life of voluntary poverty (Francis of Assisi and Mother Teresa come to mind), that sort of commitment is not a practical option for most Christians. The church's usual teaching is that poverty is a *bad* thing and that no godly purpose would be served by dramatically increasing the number of poor people in the world. Indeed, material possessions may be viewed as gifts and blessings from God, to be received and enjoyed with thanksgiving.

How, then, do we give everything to God? We do so by submitting the governance of our lives to the rule of God, to the lordship of Christ, and to the direction of the Holy Spirit.

THE RULE OF GOD

Jesus talked more about the rule of God than he did about anything else. The expression "rule of God" is often translated "kingdom of God" in our English Bibles, which is fine so long as we do not think of God's rule as being located in some particular place. Since God is everywhere, God's kingdom or rule can be found everywhere as well. Indeed, the first announcement Jesus made when he began his ministry was, "The kingdom of God has come near!" (Mark 1:14). This had nothing to do with geography. Rather, Jesus was declaring that the possibility of God ruling people's lives was near at hand. People do not have to die and go to heaven to come under God's care and to live under God's powerful rule. God is ready and willing to rule our lives here and now. Jesus called this message "the gospel" and he expected it to change people's lives, to make a difference in how they thought and behaved (Mark 1:15). Stewardship consists of living under this rule of God — and *financial* stewardship consists of placing our finances under this rule of God. Basically, the Bible says that we have a God who is ready and willing to rule our finances, and that this is good news — the sort of good news that might change our lives.

> 🕊 **We have a God who is ready and willing to rule our finances.**

The Lordship of Christ

In the early church, Christians had a simple creed: "Jesus is Lord" (see Romans 10:9). That was it — just one line. Eventually, this one-liner would need to be expanded, emphasizing that this Jesus was also "true God of true God," that he was "seated at the right hand of the Father," and so forth. Still, the essence of Christian faith has always been found in the simple recognition that Jesus is Lord. On the day of his birth, angels announced to the shepherds of Bethlehem, "To you is born this day, a Savior who is Christ the Lord" (Luke 2:11). And on the day of his return, every knee will bow and every tongue will confess "that Jesus Christ is Lord" (Philippians 2:11). To be a Christian is to be a person who names Jesus Christ as Lord. This means that Jesus Christ is in charge of our lives. We do not view such servitude as oppressive, for Jesus himself says, "Come to me all you who are weary, and I will give you rest . . . my yoke is easy, and my burden is light" (Matthew 11:28-30). We are privileged to have such a Lord and we delight in placing him in charge of our lives. But if Jesus Christ is to be lord of our lives, then he must certainly be in charge of our finances. And that is what biblical stewardship is about: we give all to God by letting Jesus Christ be lord of who we are and what we have.

The Direction of the Holy Spirit

Many Christians have difficulty talking about the Holy Spirit in ways that do not sound spooky or odd; in fact, it wasn't very long ago that we usually called the Holy Spirit the

---

🖋 What's More Important Than Giving?

Although the Bible encourages generosity, there are also many passages that indicate *something else* is more important than giving away our money:

Micah 6:6-8	justice, kindness, and humility
Matthew 5:23-24	repairing an estranged relationship
Matthew 23:23	justice, mercy, and faith
Mark 7:9-13	caring for one's family members
Luke 11:42	justice and the love of God
Luke 18:9-14	eschewing self-righteousness
1 Corinthians 13:3	love

Thus, stewardship is more than money, and faithful stewards seek to please God in how they *live* as well as how they *give*.

"Holy Ghost" (and we still do when we sing the Doxology — just because it rhymes with "host"). Different denominations have diverse ideas about how the Holy Spirit guides and directs our lives. All Christians, however, believe that there is a Holy Spirit and that this Holy Spirit *does* aid them in various ways. Jesus called the Spirit our Advocate or Helper and said that this Spirit would teach us everything (John 14:26) and guide us into all truth (John 16:13). The apostle Paul speaks of the Holy Spirit as an indwelling presence who transforms God's children from within, producing such fruit as love, joy, peace, patience, kindness, generosity, faithfulness, gentleness, and self-control (Galatians 5:22-23). Stewardship, then, may be simply a matter of allowing the Holy Spirit to direct and guide our lives, and financial stewardship may be a matter of letting the Spirit determine how we use our material resources. We open our hearts and our minds to the Spirit and ask God how we are to spend our money. No one can say for certain what answers we will receive — or how we will receive them. But merely asking the question and seeking such guidance is a significant step.

❦ *Stewardship Is 100 Percent*

ALL OF THESE CONSIDERATIONS POINT to one thing: stewardship means giving 100 percent to God. There are two reasons why Christians do not always get this. First, churches often use the phrase "giving to God" in a way that is synonymous with "giving to the church." The thought, I suppose, is that the church will serve as God's representative in receiving our gifts and using them as God would want. That may be true, but the concepts of giving to God and giving to the church should not be simply equated. There are many ways of giving our money to God, and giving to the church is only one of these. As long as we think that "giving to God" and "giving to the church" are the same thing, the concept of 100 percent stewardship will be lost on us. No one is likely to give 100 percent of their money to the church.

A second reason follows closely on the first. Churches often recognize that the summons for Christians to give up everything they own is impractical and so they modify this biblical teaching in favor of a more realistic expectation. The concept of "percentage giving," especially tithing (giving 10 percent), comes into play as one way that Christians can provide some token fulfillment of what Scripture demands. This concept does have some biblical precedent in terms of fulfilling one's responsibility to a particular religious institution (see pages 154-62), but neither tithing nor percentage giving were ever meant to serve as substitutes for the expectation that *all* of our money will be used in God-pleasing ways. The point has never been that tithers should give ten percent of their money to the church and then use the rest however they please.

When we think about "financial stewardship," then, we must not be concerned exclusively or even primarily with that portion of our money that we give to the church or to other good causes. Giving to the church is but one part of a much bigger picture. We are to consider the matter of financial stewardship in terms of what we give to **Giving to the church is but one part of a much bigger picture.** God — and God wants it all, not just a percentage. But this, again, is not to be construed primarily as an obligation or a requirement. Think of it, rather, as an invitation, as an offer from God to take charge of this often troubled area of our lives and to bring us to that place of integrity and satisfaction that the apostle Paul calls *contentment* (Philippians 4:11-12).

With regard to financial stewardship, faithful living entails at least four things: When we are faithful stewards, 1) we *acquire* our money in God-pleasing ways; 2) we *regard* our money in God-pleasing ways; 3) we *manage* our money in God-pleasing ways; and, 4) we *spend* our money in God-pleasing ways. If you are one of those persons who likes nifty acronyms, the key words here can be associated with the word *arms:*

A — Acquire

R — Regard

M — Manage

S — Spend

❧ *How We Acquire Money*

WHEN WE ARE FAITHFUL STEWARDS, we *acquire* our money in God-pleasing ways. One place to begin an evaluation of our financial stewardship is by reflecting on what we do to earn our paycheck in the first place. The Bible often shows concern for such matters.

To start with, Scripture offers no commendation for those who don't do any work at all. Everyone should "earn their own living," one text maintains, and "anyone unwilling to work should not eat" (2 Thessalonians 3:10-12). The point here is not to commend starvation for the unemployed or to put a scriptural kibosh on government-sponsored welfare programs. In context, these words were probably intended as a condemnation of the idle rich: well-to-do persons who have no need to work for a living will not be welcome at the church's community meals unless they start devoting themselves to some sort of worthwhile labor. Work is good, the Bible maintains, and even people who don't need to work for a paycheck ought to take jobs that will allow them to contribute to society and prevent them from turning into "mere busybodies" (2 Thessalonians 3:11).

Assuming that people *are* working for a living, the law of Moses provides details for honest business dealings (Leviticus 19:35-36; Deuteronomy 25:13-15), maintaining that "all who act dishonestly are abhorrent to the Lord" (Deuteronomy 25:16). The prophet Amos cries out against merchants who bring a *caveat emptor* (buyer beware) code to the marketplace by practicing "deceit with false balances" and "selling the sweepings of the wheat" (Amos 8:5-6; cf. Leviticus 19:35). In the New Testament, John the Baptist tells soldiers not to supplement their wages by extorting money or accepting bribes (Luke 3:14) and he instructs tax collectors to gather no more than the prescribed amount (Luke 3:13). Thus, scrupulous honesty is intended to typify persons who are faithful stewards of God (see also Jeremiah 17:11; Proverbs 10:2).

The Bible further indicates that money ought not be earned in ways that create hardships for those who can least afford them. God forbids the Israelites from taking advantage of those who "have fallen into difficulty," saying, "Do not take interest in advance or otherwise make a profit from them" (Leviticus 25:35-37; see also Exodus 22:25-27). The prophet Amos rails against those who gain wealth at the expense of the poor (Amos 2:6-7; 5:11). In the New Testament, Jesus castigates religious leaders who have become rich by confiscating the homes of widows

(Luke 20:47) and his brother James has some choice words
for wealthy landowners who fail to pay their field hands a
decent wage (James 5:1-6).

Beyond these somewhat obvious concerns for earning wages with honesty and integrity, the Bible reveals a
deeper concern for acquisition of finances: it is never to
become an end in itself. The prophet Isaiah issues a stern
warning to "you who join house to house, who add field to
field, until there is room for no one but you, and you are
left to live alone in the midst of the land" (Isaiah 5:8). Thus,
an accumulation of material things must not dominate
one's life to the extent that one does not even use or enjoy
what one has. Jesus' parable of the rich fool (Luke 12:16-
21) offers a classic description of someone who does not
understand that "life does not consist in the abundance of
possessions" (Luke 12:15). Jesus also asks a probing question in Mark 8:36-37: would it be worth gaining the entire
world, if you had to give up your *life?* He is not just referring
here to physical death, but to a "loss of life" that can constitute the hidden cost of success. A big paycheck ceases to be
of much value if earning it involves giving up what makes
life worthwhile: faith, time, relationships, family, peace of
mind, and so forth.

The workplace in our modern world is fraught with
temptations and challenges to biblical teaching: it may
be commonplace in many sectors to take advantage of a
client's naïveté, to exaggerate a product's potential, to seek
the destruction or disparagement of competitors, or to
cover up matters that defraud employers or constituencies.
We may also live and work in a culture that shows cavalier

disregard for the collateral damage our personal gains inflict upon others and that views the acquisition of wealth as a worthy goal in its own right. Being a Christian in a non-Christian world is complicated, but this is where our commitment to financial stewardship begins. The good news is that we can submit ourselves to living in accord with the will of God and trust that God will guide us in discerning what is right (Proverbs 3:5-6; Micah 6:8; James 1:5). We also know that God will take care of us even if our ethical commitments cause us to forgo the "winning formulas" that promise maximum success according to the standards of our age (Philippians 4:19). Such standards come and go, but the Bible contains wisdom that has endured for almost three millennia:

> *Better is a little with fear of the Lord*
> *than great treasure and trouble.*
> *Better is a dinner of vegetables where love is*
> *than a fatted ox and hatred....*
> *Better is a little with righteousness*
> *than large income with injustice....*
> *Better to be poor and walk in integrity*
> *than to be crooked and rich. (Proverbs 15:16-17; 16:8; 28:6)*

Stewards of God, however, do not just seek to avoid what is negative, resisting temptations to dishonesty, sloth, or greed. Beyond that, we are encouraged to view our employment positively as a vocation from God, as something that we do in order to make a worthy contribution to life in this world. Perhaps no one has said this more clearly than

Martin Luther. In Luther's day, most people believed that religious occupations were of a higher order than secular ones, that persons who *really* loved God or were exceptionally devoted to Christ should seek to become priests or monks or nuns. Those who pursued mundane professions — lawyers, farmers, cooks, or housekeepers — were supposedly less spiritually inclined. Luther strongly denounced this view, insisting that God calls people to do lots of different things. He encouraged every worker to view his or her job as a calling from God. This, in fact, is where we get the word *vocation,* which means "calling." The following quote is often attributed to Luther as summarizing his thinking on this matter:

> The maid who sweeps her kitchen is doing the will of God just as much as the monk who prays — not because she may sing a Christian hymn as she sweeps but because God loves clean floors. The Christian shoemaker does his Christian duty not by putting little crosses on the shoes, but by making good shoes, because God is interested in good craftsmanship.

Christians are responsible stewards when they do something worthwhile for a living, regardless of whether the activity is specifically religious. Of course, there may be some professions that stewards of God should simply avoid, work that is intrinsically immoral or contrary to the purposes of God. Luther himself thought this of certain "trading companies" of his day, which he called "a bottomless pit of avarice and wrongdoing." His only advice to Christian employees of these hopelessly corrupt companies was "Get out! They will not change." But, generally speaking, we can all be faithful stewards of God by pursuing occupations that involve us in useful and worthwhile activities.

How We Regard Money

WHEN WE ARE FAITHFUL STEWARDS, we *regard* our money in God-pleasing ways. The Bible often displays strong interest in the attitudes and motivations that undergird human behavior, and this is never more true than with regard to material things.

The first thing we should note is that the Bible generally encourages us to take a *positive* attitude toward our possessions. God is often identified as the ultimate source of prosperity: "whoever trusts in the Lord will be enriched" (Proverbs 28:25). Jesus himself says that the Father in heaven gives "good things" to his children (Matthew 7:11) and we might conclude from other stories in the Gospels that such good things include not only the gift of the Holy Spirit (Luke 11:13) or forgiveness of sins (Luke 1:77), but also nice clothes and jewelry (Luke 15:22), fatted calves (Luke 15:23), casks of wine (John 2:6-10), perfume (Mark 14:3-6), houses and fields (Mark 10:30) and other things associated with pleasant living in a very material world.

Christians are responsible stewards when they do something worthwhile for a living.

In the Old Testament, Moses specifically commands the

Israelites to view affluence as something to celebrate: "You shall eat your fill and you shall bless the Lord your God for the good land that he has given you" (Deuteronomy 8:10). But this encouragement is accompanied by a warning, by words that are so timeless in their relevance that they could almost be addressed to modern Americans:

> When you have eaten your fill and have built fine houses and live in them, and when your herds and flocks have multiplied, and your silver and gold is multiplied, and all that you have is multiplied . . . Do not say to yourself, "My power and the might of my own hand have gotten me this wealth." But remember the Lord your God, for it is he who gives you power to get wealth. (Deuteronomy 18:12-14, 17-18)

THE PROBLEM WITH AFFLUENCE, THEN, is not that there is anything wrong with prosperity itself but that material abundance often leads to spiritual amnesia.

How are we are to regard our money in ways that entail "remembering the Lord"? Despising wealth is clearly not an option for those whose God gives them power to get wealth. But Scripture does say that "the *love* of money is the root of all kinds of evil" (1 Timothy 6:10). And Jesus says, "You cannot *serve* God and wealth" (Matthew 6:24). Money, then, is not to be something that we love or serve — it is to be something that we *use.* Or, to say it differently, we should not allow money to become the prime source of joy and meaning in our lives (that would be loving it) nor should we allow money to exercise a controlling influence over us (that would be serving it).

Having said this, I want to focus on two attitudes that particularly characterize faithful stewards: gratitude and trust.

GRATITUDE

A grateful person is one who has a deep sense of life as a gift and, so, appreciates and enjoys life much more than he or she would otherwise. Fulton Oursler (author of *The Greatest Story Ever Told*) recalls wondering as a child why the family gave thanks for their food at every meal when, as near as he could tell, they would have gotten the food whether they gave thanks for it or not. Anna, the servant woman responsible for his care, told him, "It makes everything taste better to be thankful" (*Behold This Dreamer*, p.13).

Stewards are encouraged to view their material possessions as gifts of God and to be thankful for them. With all of the Bible's warnings against storing up treasure on earth (Matthew 6:19), it might be easy to go overboard and end up despising material things as inherently ungodly. But Jesus himself enjoyed a good banquet (Matthew 11:19) and appreciated having costly ointment poured over his feet (Mark 14:3-6). He acknowledged that life is "more than food, and the body more than clothing" (Matthew 6:25) but nevertheless claimed that food and clothing were good things given by God for our enjoyment (Matthew 6:23-30; 7:11). We are not to despise such things — but we are not to think that we are *entitled* to them either, as though the world simply "owes us a living." In our modern age, notions of entitlement run rampant and have become increasingly easy to adopt. Such notions are a surefire prescription for joyless living: we find it difficult to appreciate what we have when we think that we are only getting our due, and we find it easy to complain about what we lack when we think that we are *not* getting our due.

The good news of biblical stewardship provides an antidote to entitlement. It inculcates genuine gratitude, a first cousin to joy. G. K. Chesterton says, "Gratitude is the true test of happiness" (*Orthodoxy,* p. 55). Those who view life as a gift and who receive all things, including life itself, with gratitude are likely to be the happiest people on earth. Among their number are faithful Christian stewards who realize that everything comes from God and who view their material goods as unmerited blessings to be received with glad and grateful hearts.

TRUST

Acknowledgment of God as the giver of all that we have implies trust in God's continuing benevolence. Such trust is the antithesis of anxiety. The Bible cautions us not to be anxious, not even with regard to the basic necessities of life (Matthew 6:25-33). "Do not worry about tomorrow," Jesus says quite plainly (Matthew 6:34). "Do not worry about *anything*," the apostle Paul adds, but "with thanksgiving, let your requests be made known to God" (Philippians 4:6). Such counsel seems remarkably relevant for our modern era, an age in which conveniences have provided no safe haven from stress. As we all know, stress is not only unpleasant and harmful to one's emotional well-being, but is unhealthy in other respects as well and can even be life-threatening. Two thousand years ago, Jesus and Paul prescribed the only known antidote for stress: *trust.* Again, we might see why the biblical message of stewardship is good news. When we are faithful stewards, trusting in God to provide us with what we need, we will have better and more satisfying lives.

We can go deeper and recognize that trust implies not only an absence of something negative (anxiety) but also the cultivation of something positive. It yields *content-ment,* that wonderful sense of sufficiency or satisfaction to which we have made reference previously (pages 41-42). It is trust in God that accounts for the apostle Paul's startling claim, "I have learned to be content with

> 🎵 **When we are faithful stewards, trusting in God to provide us with what we need, we will have better and more satisfying lives.**

whatever I have" (Philippians 4:11). In like fashion, we not only trust God that we *will* have enough to get by; we trust God that we *do* have enough, already, right now. We have enough to be the people God wants us to be and to have the lives God wants us to have. In saying this, I do not mean to imply that there is anything wrong with keeping a "wish list" of things that we would someday like to have. I also think that it is natural and appropriate to hope that our material standard of living might improve as we progress through life. Still, if we think that we will be happier or better people when that happens, we may be deceived.

Trust is not only an antidote to anxiety but is also our best defense against *greed,* against the insatiable desire always to have more. We live in a society where more than 50 billion advertising dollars are spent each year to make us cravers of things that we do not own. And even without those advertisements, many of the products are intrinsically desirable, items that would appear to make our lives easier, more meaningful, or simply more delightful. Sometimes, of course, the appearance is a false one — the products don't deliver what the advertisements promise — but this is not always the case. Most of us have bought things — mere *things* — that really did make our lives easier, more meaningful, or more delightful. We live in an age of wonders, an age in which there appears to be a limitless supply of things that we would not only like to own but that, with just a little more money, we probably could own. This combination of "desirable" and "potentially obtainable" becomes a constant lure, and it is perhaps the *constancy* of the lure that turns desire into a lifestyle — and when desire becomes a lifestyle it earns the label "greed." We get caught in an addictive spiral of spending, acquiring more and more while feeling like we have less and less. This is not just a vice; it is a form of captivity.

We should also say a word about one form of greed that thrives in any society based on competition: envy, or what the Bible calls covetousness. Everyone knows that the Bible commands us not to covet (it is one of the Ten Commandments, after all), and everyone realizes that envy is

an undesirable trait (no one ever *seeks* to become envious).
Nevertheless, envy and covetousness seem to run rampant
in our contemporary world. We may be compelled to dis-
satisfaction in life because even when we do think that we
"have it good," we are bothered by the thought that someone else may "have it better." Jesus once told a parable
about this (Matthew 20:1-15): God is like an employer who
is generous with everyone; still, some workers complain
that he is *more* generous with others than he is with them.
Jesus does not use the parable as an occasion for disput-
ing whether this is the case. Rather, the story portrays the
employer as stopping those grumblers in their tracks with
a simple question: "Am I not allowed to do what I choose
with what belongs to me?" God will give to us generously,
and that's all we need to know; beyond that, God can give
to any and to all as God wishes and it is, quite frankly, none
of our business if God chooses to give more generously to
others than to us. Likewise, in a completely different parable, Jesus compares God to a master who gives his servants different numbers of talents (Matthew 25:14-30): one
gets ten, another gets five, a third gets only one. The point
of the story seems to be that God does not distribute gifts
or resources with monotonous uniformity and the very fact
of this serves as a reminder that they are God's to give.

The good news of biblical stewardship starts with the
realization that all things come from God and are God's to
give as God chooses. This is *good* news because we know
that God is generous and loving, that God knows us better than we know ourselves, and that God will do what is
right for us. For Paul, the secret of being content seems to

lie in an absolute assurance that God provides him with everything he needs to be the person God wants him to be and to have the life that God wants him to have. And that is enough. It does not matter one whit if someone else has more, for he trusts that what he has is right for *him.* God provides him with whatever is sufficient for him to have the best possible life that he can have in this world. Trust in this generous and perceptive God yields contentment, which makes for a much more pleasant life than one consumed by greed or covetousness.

❦ *How We Manage Money*

WHEN WE ARE FAITHFUL STEWARDS, we *manage* our money in God-pleasing ways. The Bible has more to say about money management than we might suppose. Of course, the world of the Bible knew nothing of stock markets, tax brackets, or pension plans. We cannot expect detailed advice for our modern world and it is not the purview of this book to offer the kind of detailed counsel that is readily available in many other volumes. As a general principle, though, we may note that the Bible indicates money is to be *used,* not hoarded. The best example of this may be the parable of the rich fool that Jesus tells in Luke 12:15-21. This man has so many goods that his barns will not hold them. His biggest problem in life is what to do with all his stuff. So, he finally hits upon a solution — tear down the barns and build bigger ones. Note his reasoning: "I need bigger barns," not "I need less stuff." But he is going to die and discover the truth of that old adage, "You can't take it with you" (see Psalm 49:17; 1 Timothy 6:7). Or, as we used to say in Texas, "There is a reason why you never see a hearse pulling a U-Haul."

There is another problem that we also want to avoid. The opposite of *hoarding* may be *squandering,* and the Bible does not denounce the former so as to recommend the latter. Indeed, just three chapters after the parable of the rich fool, we find a story about a foolish boy who squanders his inheritance on frivolous pursuits and then is caught unawares when a famine comes upon the land (Luke 15:12-16). So, saving money for some definite purpose is not the same as storing away more than we ever intend to use. To get this right, to avoid both *hoarding* and *squandering,* we need to have a plan . . . indeed, a *budget.* We need to think through our intentions and prayerfully submit them to God, asking, "How much should I set aside for this or for that? When am I storing away too much and when am I saving too little?"

Jesus told yet another parable that commends such faithfulness. In Matthew 25:14-30, he speaks of a man who gives money to three of his servants and waits to see what they will do with what they have been given. Two of the servants are deemed "good and trustworthy" because they successfully engage in the commerce of the day and manage to double what was given them. The third servant is denounced because he simply buries the money in the ground and digs it up later, proud that nothing was lost. Like most parables, this story has a wide range of applications, but there is certainly something to be learned with regard to financial counsel. Faithful stewardship involves wise management of our finances and doing *nothing at all* is seldom the best course.

Concern for money management is one of the most overlooked areas in contemporary stewardship. Churches often want to talk to their members about responsible use of their available income, emphasizing scriptural calls to help the poor, feed the hungry, and support religious institutions. This is all well and good but many members who might want to do such things are unfortunately trapped in spirals of indebtedness that make noble ambitions hard to fulfill. To be blunt, the poor choices that they have made with regard to managing their money can impede their best intentions regarding how they might now like to use it. Once the bills are paid, there just isn't enough "available income" left to use in all those wonderful ways that the church commends. Some bills, of course, are inevitable, but others are not, and it is often the unnecessary ones that drain our resources the most. To take but one, obvious example, the pervasiveness of high-interest credit-card debt in our modern society is evidence that mismanagement of personal finances has reached epidemic proportions.

"Owe no one anything, except to love one another," the apostle Paul once said (Romans 13:8). If we want to be able to use our money as God would want, we need to stay clear of frivolous and avoidable debt. For many of us, faithful stewardship must begin with a basic commitment to getting our finances under control. Faithful stewardship means altering our spending habits, developing a budget, and learning to invest and save our money wisely. It means seeking the counsel of trained financial advisors, and approaching all of our decisions about money management with prayerful consideration of what God would have us do.

✖ How We Spend Money

WHEN WE ARE FAITHFUL STEWARDS, we *spend* our money in God-pleasing ways. This, I suppose, is what most people think is the crux of the matter, though different people may have different ideas as to what it means to spend our money in God-pleasing ways. John Westerhoff suggests the following:

> Stewardship is about giving up the love of possessing and practicing a life of simplicity; of developing the habit of giving things away; of buying only what is absolutely necessary; of rejecting anything to which we are becoming addicted; of learning to enjoy things without owning them; of developing a greater appreciation of and respect for the natural world; of rejecting anything that will result in an injustice for others. (*Grateful and Generous Hearts*, pp. 33-34)

YOUR PRIORITIES MAY VARY, BUT what should not be controversial is that biblical stewardship involves not only responsibility to God but also to other people and, indeed, to ourselves. We often love God best by showing love for our neighbor and by exercising appropriate self-care. God blessed Abraham so that he could be a blessing to others (Genesis 12:2) and in keeping with that thought, the New Testament teaches that "good stewards of the manifold grace of God" will use what God gives them in ways that serve others (1 Peter 4:10-11).

I hope that we can now realize some of the implications of what we have been saying all along: stewardship is 100 percent. All that we are and all that we have belongs to God. Therefore, we are to use *all* of our money in ways that fall appropriately under the heading "giving to God." We are to use *all of it* in ways that will please God, in ways that demonstrate our devotion to the rule of God, the lordship of Christ, and the direction of the Holy Spirit.

The resistance that I often get from people at this point can be quite revealing. Indeed, it is revealing in two different ways. First, there are some people who simply reject the notion of 100 percent stewardship outright. Perhaps they are only willing to make a token allegiance to Christ, or perhaps they just think that giving God a portion or a certain percentage of their resources should be sufficient. At any rate, they are not willing to recognize God as owner of all that they have or to accept the implications of such sovereignty. I am not sure what to say to such persons except to tell them that they are wrong and that they need to repent. I have said above that many Christians speak about two types of preaching: law and gospel. The stubborn and the impenitent need to hear the law: clear statements of what God requires. The guilt-

We often love God best by showing love for our neighbor.

ridden and the fearful need to hear the gospel: unequivocal proclamations of God's grace and mercy. Like most preachers, I have always preferred proclaiming gospel to law, but if you are a person who is only willing to give God a part of your life (or your finances), then you need for someone to give you the tough talk. God either rules your life or God doesn't. Jesus is not interested in being your lord on Sunday mornings only. The Holy Spirit does not come into your life to help you with a few selected problems while leaving everything else alone. The bottom line for all of us is that if we want to be children of God and followers of Jesus Christ then we must recognize that we are not ultimately owners but stewards — stewards of what belongs to God. And God does hold us accountable for what we do with that which is entrusted to us — all of it!

But often the resistance to the notion of 100 percent stewardship comes from another direction: Sometimes Christians will acknowledge the basic truth of what has just been said and adopt a certain guilt-ridden willingness to try to use all of their money as God wants, but they do this with a heavy heart and an ominous sense of what they assume it means. This is also revealing, for their assumptions indicate what they believe about God. "The thing is, I like to spend some of my money on myself," one person complained. He apparently thought that God would be pleased when he spent money on other people, including his friends and his family, but that God would not want him to spend money on himself. "I don't want to do just religious things all the time," someone else told me. Indeed, a woman in one of my Sunday school classes said that if she took this seriously (using all of her money in God-pleasing ways) she would have to give up one of her chief joys in life — going to musicals and concerts. "I'll just have to listen to all that Christian music," she said, "which isn't nearly as good." So, is that the kind of God that you think we have? A God who is only happy when people think religious thoughts and do religious things and listen to religious music? People with this notion of God, I think, need to hear the preaching of the gospel, they need to hear the *good news* that God loves people and wants them to be happy. God wants us all to have abundant and joyful lives.

It is true that Christian stewardship generally commends the virtue of *frugality,* a way of moderation that encourages Christians to distinguish between luxuries and necessities and to place some limits on acquisition of the former. But not everyone will agree that Christians should buy "only what is absolutely necessary" (as Westerhoff suggests above). John Schneider, for instance, extols the inherent delight of "getting behind the wheel of a fine-tuned car . . . curling up in a pleasurable sitting room in front of a fire . . . or grilling steaks on a cedar deck on a warm spring evening" (*The Good of Affluence,* p. 61). Such expressions of the basic goodness of life may be rightly enjoyed as God's blessings — and relatively affluent Christians should not be constantly made to feel guilty for having good things that others may lack.

There are some who pursue frugality or moderation on the basis of the law but without any recognition of the gospel. A writer in Proverbs pleads, "Give me neither poverty nor riches. . . . Or, I shall be full and deny you. . . .

Or, I shall be poor and steal" (Proverbs 30:7-9). Such thinking is grounded in fear and espouses a "damned if you do,
damned if you don't" attitude toward stewardship. The
apostle Paul, as we have seen, evinces exactly the opposite
approach: Rich or poor, having plenty or little . . . it doesn't
matter. He knows that he will be content and that he will
be a faithful steward of Jesus Christ regardless (Philippians
4:12). He knows that his faithfulness in stewardship is not
ultimately dependent upon his own efforts but upon the
power of God. Paul does not assume that either poverty or
riches would be his undoing because he knows that God
is at work in him (Philippians 1:6) and that he can do all
things through Christ (Philippians 4:13).

Accordingly, Christians may view the commendation of
frugality and moderation not as a requirement of the law
but as an invitation to a joy-filled life. We all know that acquisition of possessions does not in itself bring joy. What is
called for, then, is not an arbitrary distinction between "necessities" and "luxuries" but discernment regarding what
is truly worthwhile and what is not. Ultimately, such decisions must be matters for personal conscience or family
discussion. The answers that Christian stewards give may
not always be consistent or predictable, but the mere fact
that they consider such matters prayerfully, seeking the
guidance of God's Spirit, will set them apart from the general population. Paul says, "Do not be conformed to this
world, but be transformed by the renewing of your minds,
so that you may discern what is the will of God — what is
good and acceptable and perfect" (Romans 12:2). People
who think and pray about how to use their money in God-

pleasing ways will be non-conformists in the sense that
Paul speaks. They will be transformed people with renewed
minds, and God will grant them the discernment that they
seek (see also James 1:5).

If we begin consciously spending our money in ways
that we believe are pleasing to God, we will not miss out on
the pleasures of life. If anything, we will begin appreciating
such pleasures all the more, knowing that God approves
and applauds our enjoyment of this good world and much
that it affords. Discerning people lack no appreciation for
the wonder and value of life but, to the contrary, appreciate what they have and do not regret the absence of what
they choose to forgo. We
need make no apologies for
showing such discernment.
Westerhoff points out, for
instance, that parents often
deflect the more extravagant
desires of their children by
saying, "We can't afford that."

> If we begin con-
sciously spending our
money in ways that we
believe are pleasing to
God, we will not miss out
on the pleasures of life.

The implicit message is that the parents *would* buy the
costly item if they had the money, which may or may not
be true. In any case, the children are left feeling sad and,
worse, believing that such sadness could be remedied if
only the family had more money. Why not tell the children,
"We don't think that getting this would be a good use of our
money" or even, "We don't believe that God would want us
to use our money in this way"? Of course, such a response
might invite arguments from the children regarding why
the purchase *would* be a good use of the family's money

or why God *would* favor the purchase, but such discussions involve the entire family in thinking about the use of money in broader terms than "Can we afford it?" (see p. 20 of Westerhoff's book *Grateful and Generous Hearts*).

The most important point here may be a simple recognition that using our money as faithful stewards of God involves more than just giving to churches, charities, and other worthy causes. As we will see in the next chapter, God definitely wants us to give some of our money away, but God is also interested in what we do with the *rest* of our money. As faithful stewards, we want to use all of our money in ways that are pleasing to God.

Stewardship and the Church

MOST PEOPLE FIRST HEAR THE word *stewardship* in association with money and in connection with their local church. Many Christian churches have a stewardship committee that is responsible for seeing that the budget needs of the church are met. Many churches also sponsor a Stewardship Sunday or an annual stewardship campaign devoted to persuading members to give more generously in support of the church's mission and programs. All of this may be good and necessary (Romans 12:8, 13), but I hope we realize by now that there is more to stewardship than just making sure that the church's financial needs are met. A full stewardship program in a local congregation might feature lots of things that are not directly related to that concern.

> ### 🖋 How Much Should I Give?
>
> From the point of view of the gospel, the very question "How much should I give?" indicates a spiritual immaturity marked by legalistic calculation instead of the overflowing spontaneity of the faith that works through love. It is the same type of question as Peter's question, "How often should I forgive my brother?" (see Matthew 18:21-22). On that level, "one-tenth" is as reasonable an answer to the question of giving as Peter's suggestion of "seven" is to the question of forgiving. The Lord's answer to Peter's question, "Not seven, but seventy times seven," indicates that his answer as to how much to give would be, "Not one-tenth, but ten times one-tenth."
>
> *T. A. Kantonen,* A Theology for Christian Stewardship, *p. 24.*

The church's stewardship committee might sponsor programs on vocational discernment or business ethics to help parishioners determine whether they are acquiring their money in ways that are pleasing to God. The pastor might offer a series of sermons or Bible studies encouraging gratitude and trust as attitudes that mark the way faithful stewards regard their material resources. The congregation might identify capable persons among its membership who would be willing to meet with those struggling to manage their money responsibly, advising them on such things as budget planning, spending restrictions, and basic investment strategies. The Adult Sunday School forum could entertain lively discussions concerning how faith can impact the decisions Christians must make when they are committed to spending all of their money in ways that are pleasing to God. And we have only scratched the surface.

Remember — in this book, we are talking primarily about *financial* stewardship. The congregation could also have programs related to stewardship of the earth (water conservation, recycling), care of our physical bodies (nutrition, health), time management, and much, much more.

Stewardship is a matter of *faithful living,* of recognizing that all we are and all we have belongs to God and is to be given to God as an act of worship, as an expression of faith, and as a spiritual discipline through which we commit our hearts in love and praise. Such faithful living is a response to the gospel, a recognition of the good news that the rule of God has come near, that Jesus Christ is our Lord, and that the Holy Spirit will direct and guide us to be the people God wants us to be and to have the abundant, joyful lives that God wants us to have.

Discussion Questions

1. Think about how you *acquire* your money: Is God pleased with your vocation and with what you do to make a living?

2. Think about how you *regard* your money: How can you cultivate an attitude of gratitude and trust, rather than entitlement, anxiety, or greed?

3. Think about how you *manage* your money: Do you think that you have found the right balance between "hoarding" (storing away too much) and "squandering" (saving too little)? Which problem poses the greatest struggle for you?

4. Think about how you *spend* your money: What do you think of the concept of "100 percent stewardship" — is it realistic to use *all* of your money as God would want? What changes would you have to make to do that?

5. How has your church been helpful to you in sorting out these four areas of "faith and money." In which area have you received the most help from your church — and in which have you received the least?

CHAPTER FIVE

Faithful Giving

It is more blessed to give than to receive.

Acts 20:35

THIS CHAPTER DOES NOT TREAT a new topic, but one specific aspect of what we are already discussing. Faithful *giving* is part of faithful *living* — it is one way of using our finances in a manner that is pleasing to God. In a sense, it is only one way among many, and yet it is a highly significant way that merits special attention.

Why is this subject so important? There is not necessarily anything more spiritual or godly about giving money to a church or to any other cause than there is about paying bills, buying a new suit, sending children to college, or saving for retirement. God may be equally pleased with us for using our money in any of these ways. What makes giving to a church or charity special is the aspect of *renunciation.* We take a portion of our money and we give it *away.* We completely give it away for *others* to use in what we hope will be a God-pleasing manner.

The spiritual principle of renunciation is important in

the Bible and is clearly presented in the stories of Jesus.
The Gospels consistently tell of Jesus calling his followers
to renounce worldly goods and material possessions. His
disciples leave their boats and nets to fish for people (Mark
1:18, 20; 10:28). Levi leaves his tax office (Mark 2:14), and
even blind Bartimaeus leaves his coat (Mark 10:50). Jesus
likens entering God's kingdom to giving up one's belongings in order to obtain a precious treasure (Matthew 13:44-
45) and he directs a rich man to sell his possessions and
give the money to the poor (Matthew 19:21). Such direc-
tives may seem extreme but, certainly, Jesus calls all of his
followers to deny themselves (Mark 8:34) and to resist the
temptation of storing up treasure on earth (Matthew 6:19).

The basic point seems to be that we have a *need* to give.
Stewardship, then, is not just about our meeting the needs
of the poor, or the needs of our church, or the needs of
any particular charity — it is about fulfilling our own need
to give as well. Accordingly, church members are often
told, "Give from the heart, not to a budget!" Don't give just
because the church needs your money; give because your
heart is filled with faith and hope and love for God.

While this is certainly true, I think that the matter can
be overstated. In addition to relating instances of Jesus is-
suing a spiritual call for renunciation, the New Testament
contains several passages that record the joys and struggles
of early church leaders in dealing with monetary concerns.
Bills need to be paid: one may think of this as a mundane
matter but it is not to be ignored. Giving from the heart
rather than to a budget sounds nice, but pastors need to be
paid whether their parishioners feel good about God each

week or not. Mortgage companies and utilities do not offer payment plans geared to how grateful or generous a congregation's membership is feeling in any particular month. So in this chapter (and the two that follow) we will try to hold together two facets of Christian giving: as believers in Jesus Christ we are invited by the gospel and empowered by God to 1) support the needs of our local congregation and 2) make meaningful sacrifices through renunciation of worldly goods. To put it simply, faithful stewardship is a duty *and* a delight: it involves both giving to the budget *and* from the heart, and it is God's grace that inspires and enables us to do both of these things.

✥ *The New Testament Church*

IN THE NEW TESTAMENT, GIVING to the church seems to encompass at least four concerns. First, there is a general expectation that ministers will be supported by the people they serve. Paul may have sometimes practiced a tent-making style of ministry (supporting himself through a secondary vocation), but he describes this as an exception to the Lord's commandment that "those who proclaim the gospel should get their living by the gospel" (1 Corinthians 9:14). Even though he gives up his own right to be paid a salary, he clearly does not think that this should be a normative expectation for most ministers (1 Corinthians 9:3-18).

Second, there is widespread concern to provide for members of one's congregation who are in need. In the first days after Pentecost, believers eschewed the very idea

of private ownership and pooled their possessions so that
there would not be a needy person among them (Acts 2:44-
45; 4:32-35). Later, the focus seems to have shifted to voluntary charity but the concern was no less strong. James de-
fines "religion that is pure and undefiled" as being "to care
for widows and orphans in their distress" (James 1:27).
And, he continues, "If a brother or sister is naked and lacks
daily food, and one of you says to them, 'Go in peace; keep
warm and eat your fill,' and yet you do not supply their
bodily needs, what is the good of that?" (James 2:15-16).

A third concern for giving in the New Testament is support for *other* communities of faith that might be in distress. This is most evident in the collection for Jerusalem
that we hear about in Acts 11:29-30 and in Paul's letters
(Romans 15:25-27; 1 Corinthians 16:1-4; 2 Corinthians 8–9).
We will say more about this collection later, but apparently
the church in Jerusalem had endured some sort of crisis
and now other churches throughout the Roman Empire
were collecting funds to meet that church's needs. What
strikes me as especially noteworthy about this collection is
that the church of Jerusalem was led by James, a man with
whom Paul had serious differences. Paul somewhat grudg-
ingly acknowledges James as a leader within the church
(see Galatians 2:6, 9) but he also claims that all had been
well at his own church in Antioch until "certain people
from James" interfered and caused problems (Galatians
2:11-14). Thus, there were theological and political dis-
putes between Paul and James not too dissimilar from
those that divide Christianity into various denominations
today. The picture of Paul going throughout the world

collecting money for the church in Jerusalem (headed by James) is not unlike a denomination in today's world spearheading a fund-raising effort on behalf of a rival sect. Imagine if the United Methodist Church were to decide that its primary stewardship emphasis for the next year would be raising money to give to the Southern Baptists! Or vice-versa, of course.

Finally, there is concern within the New Testament for the funding of worldwide mission and evangelism. Already in the Gospels, we discover that the ministry of Jesus is in part sustained through the generosity of numerous women who use their resources to provide for him (Luke 8:1-3). And when Jesus sends his disciples out as missionaries, he says that their basic needs should be provided for them and that God will hold accountable those who do or do not provide such support (Matthew 10:9-15, 40-42; 25:31-46). Such programs would continue and expand in the days to come, with an obvious expectation that continued support would be necessary. If the church is to proclaim the good news of the kingdom throughout the world (Matthew 24:14) and make disciples of all nations (Matthew 28:19), someone will have to foot the bill for travel expenses. Beyond this concern for evangelism, furthermore, Christians seem from the very first to have felt called to care for the poor and needy of the world as, indeed, Jesus had directed (Luke 14:12-14). The first order of business may have been caring for needy persons within the church itself but no one ever seems to have thought that this was enough (see Galatians 6:10). Jesus said the church was to be "the salt of the earth" and "light for the world" (Matthew 5:13-14) and he indicated that his gospel was good news for the poor, period, not just good news for poor Jews or poor Christians (Luke 4:16-28). He said that there is nothing special about people who give generously and do good to their own kind (Luke 6:33); his followers were to be known as the people who give to everyone and who do good to all, even to those who hate them (Matthew 5:42-48; Luke 6:30-36). His parable of the generous Samaritan illustrates precisely this point: those who understand what Jesus means by "love your neighbor" will open their purses and use their money to meet the needs of people who do not affirm or even respect their religion (Luke 10:33-35).

Church budgets in our present day may display attention to some or all of these concerns, but they also reveal that matters have gotten quite a bit more complicated. Most congregations in our modern world have outgrown the capacity for meeting in the homes of members, as congregations often did in New Testament times (Acts 2:2, 46; 12:12; 20:20). Thus, buildings are required — and all of the expenses that come with them: land, utilities, maintenance, upkeep. Most churches sponsor educational programs, requiring the purchase of materials and equipment. Many congregations print newsletters and send out mailings to their members and/or others in the community. We may bemoan the fact that things are not as simple as they once were (or appear to have been), but a church in the twenty-first century cannot be (nor should it be) just

> ✒ **We are here to glorify God and to advance the gospel of Jesus Christ through word and deed.**

like a church in the first century. Our task is to be faithful to New Testament teaching within the context of our own era. We do this, I think, by keeping the focus of finances on mission and benevolence, and by developing budgets that, for all their elaboration, remain true to these purposes. We are here to glorify God and to advance the gospel of Jesus Christ through word and deed. When a church develops its budget with conscious attention to those aims, we may view supporting that budget as compatible with the intent of Scripture.

✒ *Principles for Giving*

"STEWARDSHIP IS A WORD THAT conjures up very negative feelings," Douglas John Hall says. "It brings to mind the horrors of home visitations, building projects, financial campaigns, and the seemingly incessant harping of the churches for more money. Ministers cringe at the mention of Stewardship Sundays: must they really lower themselves to the status of fund-raisers once more?" (*The Steward,* p. 13).

I am sympathetic to Hall's concern, but a little bothered by his jibe at fund-raisers. Most nonprofit organizations need to rely on the services of professional fund-raisers from time to time (if not constantly) and most professional fund-raisers do their job with integrity and a minimum of manipulation, helping people to make gifts that they want to make in the manner that will be most meaningful to them and most beneficial to their recipients. Thank God

---

🖋 Stewardship and the Christian Life

W. H. Greever has indicated that the same things may be said about financial stewardship as may be said about Christianity in general:

the *motive* is love and gratitude . . .
the *purpose* is to glorify God . . .
the *guide* is the revealed will of God . . .
the *measure* is the sacrificial spirit of Christ . . .
the *efficiency* is the power of God's grace . . .
the *reward* is a good conscience and the anticipated "well done" of the Lord.

Realities in the Christian Religion *(private printing, 1951).*

---

for such fund-raisers — we need them and I do not think that they occupy a lower status than clergy on any divine scale of approved professions. But Hall's main point is that pastors and laity alike resent the approach to stewardship that we find in many churches today — an approach that often treats stewardship as though it were only a means to an end. Biblically speaking, stewardship *is* our mission, not just a means for funding our mission.

For the reasons that Hall notes, American churches often connect *giving* with *fund-raising,* which is deemed necessary for the maintenance of congregational ministries. Churches have come up with different strategies for encouraging such giving. Many churches have an annual stewardship drive, involving special sermons at Sunday services and visitation of members in their homes. At the very least, most churches today distribute offering envelopes and provide members with annual statements or records

of their giving. Quite a few also use "pledge cards," encouraging members to declare their intention ahead of time.
Some churches insist on tithing as a divinely-approved
standard for giving to the church.

The closest we get to any of this in the Bible is in certain
sections of Paul's epistles, where the apostle discusses
the aforementioned collection for the church in Jerusalem
(Romans 15:25-27; 1 Corinthians 16:1-4; and especially
2 Corinthians 8–9). Apparently that church had fallen
into hard times and the offering (taken among Gentile
churches) was intended both to help the poor and to serve
as a sign of unity between believers who came from different ethnic and cultural traditions. In any case, Paul throws
himself into the project. He is quite the unabashed fund-
raiser, and seems to regard what could have been viewed as
a peripheral or mundane matter as intrinsic to his work of
proclaiming the gospel. The very language that he uses is
interesting: Paul refers to the collection as a *charis,* using
the Greek word for *grace* or *gift* (translated "generous un-
dertaking" by the New Revised Standard Version in 2 Corinthians 8:6 and 8:19). He also refers to it as a "eulogy"
(Greek *eulogia,* translated "bountiful gift" in 2 Corinthians
9:5) and as a "liturgy" (Greek *leitourgia,* translated "ministry" in 2 Corinthians 8:12). Thus, Paul seems to think
of this collection as an act of worship through which
churches experience the love and grace of God and, in
turn, convey God's love and grace to others. He has a pretty
noble vision for what could easily have been dismissed as
mere fund-raising.

In any event, modern stewardship programs often

derive a number of basic principles regarding Christian giving from the advice that Paul gives in these portions of his letters:

1. Giving is both a duty and a delight, something we ought to do and something we are pleased to do (Romans 15:25-26).

2. Giving is to be regular and systematic, according to a plan (1 Corinthians 16:2).

3. Giving is a demonstration of God's grace (2 Corinthians 8:1; 9:14).

4. Giving need not be hampered by difficult circumstances, for even those who suffer affliction and experience poverty may exhibit generosity (2 Corinthians 8:2).

5. Giving is to be voluntary, not under compulsion (2 Corinthians 8:3; 9:5, 7).

6. Giving should be proportionate to one's income and circumstances, as each is expected to contribute according to his or her means (2 Corinthians 8:3, 11-13).

7. Giving can also be undertaken as a sacrifice, as some will feel inspired to give "beyond their means" (2 Corinthians 8:3).

8. Giving is a privilege, something we appreciate being

able to do as a result of God's grace (2 Corinthians 8:4).

9. Giving involves more than financial contributions — we first commit *ourselves* to the Lord and to the church at large (2 Corinthians 8:5).

10. Giving is a witness to the gospel, demonstrating the genuineness of the church's love (2 Corinthians 8:8, 24).

11. Giving may involve making a pledge that the giver is committed to fulfilling over time (2 Corinthians 8:10-11).

12. Giving is to represent a personal commitment — each person is to make up his or her own mind about how much to give (2 Corinthians 9:7).

13. Giving is not to be undertaken reluctantly but cheer-fully (2 Corinthians 9:7).

14. Giving is conducted in faith that God will provide for those who give (2 Corinthians 9:8-11).

15. Giving brings glory to God and leads people to give thanks to God (2 Corinthians 9:11-13).

To these might be added a few principles derived from other portions of Scripture. Jesus encourages anonymous giving, denouncing grandiose displays that call undue attention to the extravagance of donors (Matthew 6:3-4). The Old Testament encourages tithing (Malachi 3:8-10), a matter to which we shall devote some attention later (see pages 154-62). It also urges the offering of "first fruits," the discipline of giving away a portion of one's goods before using anything for oneself (Proverbs 3:9).

Obviously, there is a lot to consider here, and many books have been written on how such principles may be best incorporated into modern programs for financial stewardship in the church today. I will present my own humble effort at discerning such a program in the next two chapters, but first let us consider another fundamental matter.

Motives for Giving

WHY DO PEOPLE GIVE THEIR money to churches and other causes? The Bible says quite a bit about motives for giving and it does not approve of every motive. Psychologists have also examined various factors that motivate people to give their money away and some of those factors seem more commendable than others. We will wrap up this chapter by taking a look at some of them.

1. *To gain recognition.* Some people give money to institutions or causes in order to make themselves look good to their peers. Jesus denounces this as hypocrisy (Matthew 6:2), but it is a very human tendency. We all want to look good. To help rein in that tendency, most churches today encourage that giving be done in relative secrecy (see Matthew 6:3-4). I do *not* think this means giving records should

be kept private even from the pastor. Church leaders need to know the giving levels of their parishioners for the same reason that physicians need to know certain "vital signs" for their patients — financial giving is one key indicator of spiritual health. There is also some merit in occasional recognitions of faithfulness. Jesus publicized the extravagant generosity of one particular widow (Mark 12:41-44), and Paul bragged to the Corinthians about the generosity exhibited by the Macedonian churches (2 Corinthians 8:1-6). Of course, in those cases, neither the widow nor the Macedonians had sought such recognition — they had not given their money *in order to* obtain affirmation and praise.

2. *To attain power or influence.* Some people might be tempted to give money in order to increase their own stature or importance within the congregation or to allow them to exercise increased control over community affairs. Many congregations have experienced the "mixed blessing" of having generous members who think that the size of their donations should grant them a special role in determining the church's priorities, practices, and policies. I know of a church where a couple made a generous donation to fund the remodeling of a dilapidated room and transform it into a very nice parlor. The room was painted, carpeted, and outfitted with new furniture, all at the couple's expense. Unfortunately, the couple seemed to think that they now had the right to decide how and when this parlor should be used. They often expressed opinions about what sort of activities should be held there, subtly reminding church leaders that they had donated

the money for the church to have this parlor in the first place. In my opinion, if this couple really wanted to give their money to the church, then they ought to have given it *away,* relinquishing all control over how it would subsequently be used. In the Christian church, major givers are not supposed to have a greater say in community affairs than those who give less. The epistle of James explicitly warns against churches showing partiality toward wealthy persons, reminding them that "God has chosen the poor in the world to be rich in faith" (James 2:1-5).

3. *To appease God.* Sometimes people give to the church in an effort to curry special favor with God or to obtain forgiveness for their sins. These people are fooling themselves, for God's favor cannot be bought with money. The good news, of course, is that God's grace is available to all through faith (Ephesians 2:8). We cannot buy God, but God has bought us (1 Corinthians 6:19-20). Accordingly, we should never give out of guilt, and we do not *need* to do so, for God freely forgives all of our offenses (Romans 6:23). We should not give out of fear, and we do not *need* to do so, for God's perfect love drives out all fear (1 John 4:18). God loves us not because we are generous or love-worthy, but because God is love (1 John 4:16).

> **We should not give out of fear, and we do not *need* to do so, for God's perfect love drives out all fear.**

4. *To earn rewards.* People might be motivated to give to the church in hope that God will reward them for their

faithfulness. Giving, then, can seem more like an investment strategy than the act of sacrificial renunciation urged by Jesus. In particular, the hope that Christian giving will lead to material prosperity derives from a selfish materialism that Scripture regularly rebukes (see 1 Timothy 6:9-10 for one example). This point needs to be stressed because it is unfortunately true that a good deal of irresponsible stewardship literature has sought to appeal to human self-interest. In contrast, the prophet Amos reminds the Israelites that God's most abundant blessings were not showered upon them at a time when they were regularly paying their tithes but, rather, at a time when they were spiritually and physically lost in the wilderness, unable and probably unwilling to offer God anything at all (Amos 4:4, 5:25). With regard to divine blessings, then, we should realize that God's gifts are never for sale (Acts 8:9-14), although they are often easily attainable through prayer and supplication (Philippians 4:6).

But there is more to the matter than this. The Bible does indicate that God rewards faithfulness in matters of financial stewardship (Matthew 6:3-4; Luke 6:38; 1 Corinthians 3:14; 2 Corinthians 9:6, 11) and people who know this should not be faulted for hoping to receive what the Bible promises. The point, however, seems to be that God rewards *unselfish* faithfulness, good deeds that are performed for their own sake rather than simply as crass attempts at earning a reward. Such divine irony is captured perfectly in these words of Jesus: "Expect nothing in return, and your reward will be great" (Luke 6:35; see also Luke 14:14). Rewards for faithful stewardship are not to be viewed as compensation or remuneration for what we have done (see Luke 17:10), but as deeper extensions of grace by which those who participate in the life of Christ inevitably discover that there is no end to the unmerited favor God chooses to bestow upon them. The primary reward for faithful stewardship, furthermore, is simply having a life that is pleasing to God, for such a life is the best life that one can possibly have in this world. Faithfulness is its own reward because, when we are faithful, we experience life at its best.

5. *To fulfill an obligation.* People are often moved to give to the church out of a sense of responsibility. Perhaps they have been brought up to believe this is something they should do or maybe they just want to be obedient to the expectations of their religious leaders or to the teaching of the Bible. Such motivation is generally commendable — the Bible does present giving as something we *ought* to do (Romans 12:8, 13) and common sense dictates that people who belong to a congregation have some responsibility for supporting that body financially. The apostle Paul extols a principle of proportionate giving that will only work if everyone participates (2 Corinthians 8:10-14). By the same token, however, Paul insists that we should not give "reluctantly or under compulsion" (2 Corinthians 9:7). People should not be pressured or manipulated into giving in a way that does not reflect their personal commitments. We give because *we* believe we should, not because someone else thinks we should.

6. *To support a worthy cause.* Some people give to the church and, indeed, to other charitable organizations because they want to support programs and causes that they believe are worthwhile. Paul speaks of a congregation that begged him to be allowed to contribute to the collection he was taking up for the poor in Jerusalem (2 Corinthians 8:4). Likewise, Christians today often feel driven to donate money to a variety of good causes and they may come to think of their local congregation as one of many good causes. I think that this is basically right: it is good for people to think of their church's ministry as a cause that they want to support and it is also good for them to recognize that it may not be the *only* cause that merits their generosity. There is, however, a potential problem: helping my church to meet its budget and pay its monthly bills may not always seem as exciting or as worthwhile as feeding hungry children or funding cancer research. Yet if I give my money to other causes without contributing proportionately to my local church, other members will be forced to pay my share of the congregation's expenses for me. Such problems can easily be avoided, however, if we couple our concern for supporting worthy causes with a commitment to fulfilling basic responsibilities of church membership, and we will talk more about this later.

7. *To divest themselves of unwanted mammon.* People sometimes give away their money because it has become a burden to them, or because they fear it might become a burden to them. There is good biblical precedent for this in the words of Jesus to the rich young man who, unfortu-

nately, was unable to heed his advice (Mark 10:21-22). A happier example may be found in the story of Zacchaeus, whose divestment of property demonstrates that he is no slave to wealth (Luke 19:1-10). Likewise, there have been Christians throughout history who have felt called to rid themselves of material things that would encroach upon their spiritual priorities, and there are many in our modern world who advocate some degree of voluntary poverty as a means of maintaining solidarity with the poor. This motive for giving, then, finds approval in Scripture and in Christian tradition, though the degree of its application must be left to personal considerations — the Bible does not present any obvious or consistent standard for such divestment that could be advanced as a requirement for all.

8. *To give thanks.* People often give to the church out of gratitude for what God has done for them. "What shall I return to the Lord for all his bounty to me?" a psalmist asks (Psalm 116:12). Thanksgiving was a major impetus for offerings in ancient Israel and continues to provide a primary motivation for giving among Christians today. Paul urges generosity on the part of the Corinthians by reminding them of "the generous act of our Lord Jesus Christ" (2 Corinthians 8:9) and he concludes his instructions on stewardship by exclaiming "Thanks be to God for his indescribable gift!" (2 Corinthians 9:15). Indeed! God has done so much for us, and our giving can be a tangible sign of our gratitude. Such giving, furthermore, need not be grounded in transient emotions. Gratitude can be more than a mood — it can be a philosophy and a lifestyle. We

can adopt disciplines that express the attitude of thanksgiving and then *act* as grateful people regardless of
whether we always *feel* grateful.

9. *To express love for God.* People may also give to the
church as an expression of a love for God that goes beyond
gratitude. Giving can become an avenue for spiritual inti-
macy, a way of touching God's heart with our own. Lovers
always want to give each other gifts. Thus, we give to God
because we love God and because we want to love God

> 🎵 **Gratitude can be
> more than a mood —
> it can be a philosophy
> and a lifestyle.**

even more (see Chapter Three
of this book). Giving to the
church is only one way of "giving to God" but it *is* one way
and most people who love God
find giving to the church to be
an especially appropriate means of conveying that love.

10. *To convey the Christ within.* Finally, the ultimate motivation for giving to the church may be the transformation
that God works within us. The Bible says that we become
"new creations" in Christ — everything becomes new
(2 Corinthians 5:17). Those who abide in Christ are like
branches on a vine, bearing the fruit that he produces
through them (John 15:5). Christ lives in us (Galatians
2:20) and we become better people as God's Spirit continues its work: the grace of God makes us gracious. This
transforming work of God affects all of life, but the Bible
specifically says that one virtuous fruit the Spirit produces
in us is *generosity* (Galatians 5:22). Simply put, as God's

Spirit takes hold of us, we become more godly and, so, we become more giving, for it is the very nature of God to give (Matthew 5:45).

Here we have lots of motives for Christian giving, some positive, some negative, some spiritual, some down-to-earth. Looking at them, I am struck by something that the apostle Paul says in his letter to the Romans, when he notes how the churches in Macedonia and Achaia have shared their resources on behalf of those in need. He adds, "They were pleased to do this, and indeed they owe it to them" (Romans 15:27). In this case, giving was both something that the Christians *ought* to do and something that they *wanted* to do. It was both a responsibility and a pleasure, a duty and a delight.

Discussion Questions

1. Are you familiar with your church's budget? How is that budget developed? Do you have any say in determining how the congregation receives and spends its money?

2. Does your church's budget reflect primary attention to what is proposed here: "to glorify God and to advance the gospel of Jesus Christ through word and deed" (page 113)?

3. How does your church conduct its "stewardship program"? Is there a lot of attention to what one might call "fund-raising"? How do you feel about that?

4. Consider the fifteen principles for stewardship drawn from Paul's letters to the Romans and Corinthians (pages 116-17): which *two* of these principles do you think your congregation needs to pay the most attention to right now? Which two do you think you personally need to pay the most attention to?

5. Consider the ten "motives for giving" discussed in this chapter (pages 118-26). Which of these do you think has played the greatest part in moving you to give to the church or to other causes?

CHAPTER SIX

Support and Sacrifice

*Each of you must give as you have made up your mind,
not reluctantly or under compulsion, for God loves a
cheerful giver.*

2 Corinthians 9:7

THE POPULAR ROCK BAND Pink Floyd scored a big hit
in the 1970s with a song called "Money." It offers ironic
commentary on the attitude religious people seem to take
toward mammon: you often hear them say that "Money is
the root of all evil," but you never see them giving it away.

It's a fun song, but there are two things wrong with the
lyrics. First, informed religious people (those who know
their Bibles) realize that it is the *love* of money rather than
money itself that is the root of evil (see 1 Timothy 6:10).
And, second, people often do give it away. Religious people,
and, for that matter, many non-religious people, give away
vast amounts of money every day, week, month, and year.
They sometimes do it anonymously and they often do
it sacrificially, in ways that they cannot possibly receive
anything in return. They just give their money away, some-

times without even expecting any acknowledgment or appreciation for what they have done.

Why? What could possibly prompt seemingly sane people to give away their money? We listed some basic motives for giving in the last chapter, but now I am going to suggest that faithful giving within the church may be of two different types. The distinction is not absolute, but I think that it is helpful to discuss these two types of giving separately, in part because different motives might appropriately apply to one or the other. First, I believe that all responsible church members are called by God to support the congregations of which they are a part with reasonable contributions proportionate to their income and circumstances. Second, I think that receptive Christians will usually be moved by Scripture and the Spirit to go beyond providing such support to give up a further portion of their money as a sacrifice. Support and sacrifice: the first is our duty; the second our delight.

✺ Support

CHURCHES COST MONEY TO OPERATE and, in most cases, they must depend on the contributions of their members to meet these expenses. One duty or responsibility of belonging to a church is supporting that church financially; all church members should contribute fairly to meet the costs of the community's life and mission. As for the amount, the Bible says that everyone is to give "according to means" (2 Corinthians 8:3, 11). This means that

Christian communities are committed to egalitarianism: giving should be proportionate to one's assets (Acts 11:29; 2 Corinthians 8:12-14) and those who are able to give much are never to be esteemed above those who are only able to give a little (see Mark 12:41-44).

This responsibility may seem like something that could go without saying but, unfortunately, it cannot. I find that many church members today have never thought about this matter very intentionally and, in fact, do not even know what their proportionate share of the congregation's expenses might be. They simply go to church, take part in congregational programs, and feel that they are being generous when they put money in the offering plate. After all, such giving is purely voluntary and, if they wanted to, they could participate in church activities without giving anything at all. Still, membership in other civic organizations usually involves a fee; we don't just assume that we can belong to a club or society without paying dues or making contributions that will help the group maintain its facilities, sponsor its programs, and sustain the services that make us want to be members. Why is the church any different?

Well, there are good reasons why the church is different. The church is not a club but a living body, composed of all persons who have been made alive in God through Jesus Christ. The church is the temple of God, the abode of the Holy Spirit (1 Corinthians 3:16). The church is the bride of Christ, the beloved of the Lord awaiting joyous reunion with the Son of God who chose us before the foundation of the world (Ephesians 1:4). We are not just a club or a civic organization and we do not charge people membership dues.

Participation in the church is free, granted through
the grace and mercy of God to the totally undeserving.
Furthermore, the church of Jesus Christ does not base
its decisions regarding finances or anything else on what
seems fair or sensible by human standards. Our decisions
are guided by what accords with the wonderful promises
of God. The simple truth is that most churches have many
members who rarely contribute anything at all to their
congregation's financial
needs. Such persons are,
in effect, requiring other
members to pay their way for
them. This is not *fair* by any
human standard, but churches are communities of grace in which persons touched by
God's goodness are often willing to do far more than what
should be expected of them. Some persons give well beyond their share for the sake of those whose commitments
or abilities may be only marginal. This may not be fair but
it is good. God gives to us what we do not deserve and, in
turn, we sometimes bear the burdens of others, regardless
of whether they are worthy or appreciative or even aware
of what we are doing for them. Truth be known, most of us
have gone through times in our lives when we were on the
receiving end of such benevolence.

> *≫* **The church is not a club but a living body, composed of all persons who have been made alive in God through Jesus Christ.**

Imagine what might happen if your church began billing members regularly for their share of what the institution actually costs to operate. Some members would not be
able to pay what was requested of them. Others who could

afford it would refuse to do so, deciding in effect that if *that* is what church membership costs, then they would rather not be members after all. The poor would be humiliated, and the half-hearted driven away. It would never work.

No, *that* would never work. Churches cannot and should not charge "membership dues." What they might do, however, is educate their more committed and responsible members regarding what proportionate responsibility for the congregation's expenses actually means. Ideally, I think that most churches could follow a procedure similar to the following:

Members of the congregation who are willing and able to support the church might be asked to give their names to a financial secretary and to provide that person with some basic information regarding their financial status and circumstances (the sort of data reported on an IRS form). The financial secretary would then know a) the budget needs of the church; b) how many members are willing to help meet these budget needs; and c) the varying assets of those committed members. With this information, the financial secretary could come up with approximations for each participating member's proportionate responsibility. She or he would be able to tell each individual or family what they should seek to contribute in the next year as proportionate support for the community's life and mission together.

Such information could be communicated in a variety of ways. A general report might be published in the church newsletter, with generic statistics and examples: An individual with an annual income of y should try to contribute x. That might be sufficient, but I would actually prefer something specific and personal. What I would like is to get a letter from the church's financial secretary saying, "Mr. Powell, based on information that we have received from you and other members of this congregation, your proportionate share of the church's budget needs for this year will be *x*."

The information provided in such a letter would be useful for me to have — it would be useful spiritually and practically. If I were paying *less* than the amount quoted, I would know that other members of the church were having to pay more than their share because I was paying too little. Personally, if that were the case, I would want to know that it was the case — regardless of whether I were able or willing to do anything about it. Or if I was paying *more* than the amount quoted, well, then, I would know that at this particular point in my life I was doing alright (at least with regard to this one aspect of my life as a servant of God). I could feel good about that, give thanks to God that this was the case, and concentrate my efforts for spiritual growth in other areas. The point, obviously, would not be to encourage undue guilt or pride, but simply to let me and others know what the basic expectation of supporting the church means.

One reason that churches don't usually run their stewardship programs this way is because they think that it presents "giving to the church" as a mundane matter — people say that what I am describing sounds more like just *paying bills* than *giving to God.* I understand the objection, but I think that this just might be the point: sometimes giving to the church *is* a mundane matter and there is really no reason to spiritualize it artificially. I agree that giving to the church should be *more* than just paying bills, but we do need to get the bills paid.

I am aware that the philosophy for giving that I am now describing disagrees with most works on this subject. If there is one matter on which stewardship experts seem to have reached consensus in recent years, it is that people should give *from* their hearts rather than *to* a budget. American congregations have been taught for half a century now that they should not present their budget needs to members and then ask those members to give designated amounts to help meet those needs. The rationale for not doing so is that the best motivation for giving is love and gratitude for God rather than simply meeting obligations or helping the church to pay its bills. There is obviously something to this, but the point has taken hold so strongly that it has often been instituted in ways that deprive church members of any reliable standard for evaluating their giving. They might be naïvely contributing an amount that is far less than what they would be willing to give if only they had better information.

I know of a man — let's call him Gary — who says that he once viewed giving to the church as something like tipping in a restaurant. For several years, he regularly put five dollars in the offering plate every Sunday. Then he was asked to serve on the church council and the involvement in congregational leadership opened his eyes to what the church as an institution actually cost to operate. He also discovered that there were many people in the church who gave $200 a month and, without disclosing names,

the financial secretary told him that several of these givers
were his approximate economic peers. There were people
in the church whose income level and life circumstances
were about the same as his who regularly gave almost ten
times what he did. "Wow!" Gary told me, "I just didn't
know! It seems obvious *now* that an organization this size
can't get by on five-dollar tips, but I'd just never given the
matter much attention." There was no way that Gary could
increase his giving dramatically overnight but, over a three-
year period he was able to adjust his giving pattern to $200
a month. He went from "tipping" to supporting his church
with contributions appropriate to his means.

Basically, I think that the "give *from* the heart, not *to*
a budget" approach is correct, but it is most applicable
to the second type of giving that Christian stewards are
called to practice, the type of giving called *sacrifice,* which
we will discuss momentarily. Sacrificial giving, however,
assumes that we are already fulfilling the basic expectation of supporting our local congregation, and we do that
by contributing proportionately to the costs of community
life and mission as reflected in the budget. Thus, giving
from the heart and to the budget are not mutually exclu-
sive concepts and I am proposing that we do both. Here is
my advice: first, estimate your proportionate share of the
church's budget costs and contribute accordingly, even
if there is a sense in which it seems like just paying bills
or fulfilling an obligation. And then, once you have done
this, you will be in a position to move on to the second
type of giving and to discover what "giving from the heart"
really means.

❧ *Sacrifice*

THE NOTION OF *SACRIFICE* IS foreign to most of us today. It summons unpleasant images of violence (killing animals) and of the need for humans to appease a potentially
wrathful God. The apostle Paul, however, provides us with
a different context for considering this term when he talks
about people who give away their money cheerfully, "not reluctantly or under compulsion" but because the goodness
of God has taken hold of them (2 Corinthians 9:7). Even a
cheerful sacrifice, however, implies giving up something.

We have said that one significant feature of faithful
giving is *renunciation* — we are to use all of our money in
God-pleasing ways but we are to take some of our money
and give it away. The biblical standard for renunciation
calls for something that the world at large would regard as
radical: we relinquish control over the money that is given
and, indeed, expect nothing back in return. This is why I
treat this type of giving separately from the proportionate support that church members provide for their home
congregations. Giving to a church does not become fully
sacrificial until after the responsibility for proportionate
giving is met. Until then, we are merely doing "what we
ought to do," what might be expected of us by the most
commonsense worldly standards. There is nothing particularly radical about providing proportionate support for an
organization to which we belong; there is little renunciation or sacrifice involved in sustaining the life and mission
of our community with gifts that are fairly apportioned
according to our means.

Try to stay with me on this point, for I think that this may be the single greatest misconception regarding financial stewardship in Christian churches today: people believe that they are answering Jesus' call to sacrificial renunciation by simply fulfilling a basic expectation of responsible church membership. They have chosen to be members of a particular congregation. They want to attend the church and participate in its programs. They want to have a pastor and to benefit from the caregiving ministries that this pastor and others provide. They believe in the ideals to which the community is devoted and want to support the advancement of its concerns in the world at large. So, they give money to the church, money that is used to reduce the mortgage on the building, to pay the pastor's salary, to purchase hymnals and educational materials, to pay utility bills, and so forth. It is good and responsible that people make donations to cover these expenses — they would be wrong *not* to do so — but they are not really *giving away* their money in a sense that matches the biblical call to radical renunciation. What they are doing is fulfilling what should be a reasonable and obvious expectation of church membership — they are doing their part to sustain the life and mission of a community to which they belong.

Lest I overstate this point, let me offer a few caveats to guard against misinterpretation. I am *not* saying that our donations to a local church are offered out of self-interest, as though we were merely paying dues in exchange for services received. There are several reasons why that would not be the case. For one thing, most congregations dedicate a significant portion of their budget to benevolence, funding worthwhile programs and activities from which their own members may not directly benefit. Furthermore, any given member of a congregation will probably find that there are expenses incurred with regard to programs in which he or she does not take part. My contributions to the church may help to pay for educational materials for the children's program regardless of whether I personally have any children who use those materials. Belonging to a church means being part of a community and our contributions to the church benefit the entire community in ways that glorify God and advance the gospel of Jesus Christ (see the discussion above on pages 109-13). Thus, I have tried to be clear in saying that our proportionate support for our congregation's budget needs is, legitimately, one type of *giving.*

Having said this, however, I still think that there is a basic difference between fulfilling an expected, reasonable commitment to our local congregation and *giving away our money* in a spirit of sacrificial renunciation. I will allow that the categories overlap and I would hope to avoid casuistry in defining them. The apostle Paul speaks of those who give "according to their means" and also "beyond their means" (2 Corinthians 8:3). I'm not sure that, given a calculator, he could have determined the precise point where the one became the other. The point, however, is a spiritual one: the richest spiritual blessing — the *good news* of stewardship — is found in the arena of sacrificial giving. It is in the move from reasonable to radical (according to this world's perspective) that the goodness of God takes hold of our lives and transforms us according to the gospel. And so

I have found it helpful to evaluate my own giving in these terms: I am called by God to support my local congregation in an appropriate manner *and* I am invited by Christ to renounce mammon by giving my money away in a sacrificial sense that goes beyond the commonsense standards of what would be a reasonable expectation for me.

The principle I want to propose is this: sacrificial giving usually becomes most real *after* the basic responsibility for providing proportionate support for our church community is met. And it is this type of giving that is the proper goal of every faithful steward. It is here that we typically move beyond duty to delight. It is here that we most fully discover giving that is an act of worship, an expression of faith, and a discipline for spiritual growth.

> 𝄞 **It is in the move from reasonable to radical that the goodness of God takes hold of our lives and transforms us according to the gospel.**

The Bible teaches that we all have a spiritual need to give our money away, expecting nothing in return. *Where* we give this money is actually less important than the mere fact that we give it. This is why Jesus could praise a widow for making an offering to a religious institution that he considered to be "a den of robbers" (Mark 12:41-44; compare Mark 11:12; 12:40). She gave her money away — it was a cheerful sacrifice, and *for her* that was what mattered most in Jesus' eyes. Likewise, Jesus told a rich man to sell his possessions and give the money to the poor not just because the poor need money (though they do) but because the rich man himself needed to be set free from the hold that money had on him (Mark 10:17-27). The call for this particular individual to give up *all* of his possessions was extraordinary, but there was nothing exceptional about the basic principle involved: people find spiritual freedom through the renunciation of their possessions. This is at the heart of the good news of biblical stewardship, but it is most fully realized when we move beyond an initial (though necessary) concern for making our proportionate contribution toward meeting the budget expenses of our church.

Sacrificial giving moves us away from commonsense expectations to an enactment of what the world might regard as radical renunciation: we give money away in ways that go beyond any standard for what would be reasonable or appropriate for us, and we expect nothing in return (Luke 14:12-14). Why would anyone do such a thing? We named three reasons in the first part of this book:

1. Giving away our money is a definitive act of worship. We take something that we value and give it up as an act of devotion to God. Jesus praised a woman for pouring out a bottle of costly perfume. She had given up something she valued as an act of love for Jesus, and that is what worship is all about. We are called to do the same: to give away a portion of our money and our possessions as a sacrificial act of devotion to God.

2. Giving away our money is a demonstrable way of expressing our faith, of acting on what we believe. When we give our money away, we demonstrate that we really do believe that all things come from God and that God will

provide for our every need. Further, the literal divestment of *some* of our money enacts in a symbolic way the overall renunciation we profess with regard to *all* our material goods. We claim as Christians that Christ is Lord of all we have and that we are willing to give up everything for God; we act on this claim when we take a portion of what we value — some of our money — and completely give it away. When we do this, we put our faith into practice and discover that it is relevant and applicable to our lives in ways that inevitably turn out to be good news.

3. Giving away our money is a spiritual discipline that frees us from the inevitable pull of materialism that would draw our hearts away from God and from the things that matter most. We may have good intentions about using our money in ways that would please God, but the allure of mammon is deceitful — it will try to control us, the Bible says (see, for instance, Matthew 6:24; Mark 10:23-25). Discovering the reality of life that is "more than possessions" (Luke 12:15) requires us to put our treasures where we want our hearts to be (Matthew 6:21). The discipline of regularly taking a portion of our money and giving it away insures that we will be persons whose hearts are in the right place, whose values and commitments have not been compromised by anxiety, envy, or greed.

Faithful giving includes *renunciation* or giving our money *away.* When Jesus calls us to do this, he does not just mean that we should be financially responsible and

pay our share of the expenses incurred by communities or
organizations to which we belong. Of course we ought to
do that, but fulfilling such obvious commitments is not
what Jesus means when he tells us to give our money away.
He means that we are to practice a special type of giving
that goes beyond commonsense expectations to involve
what the world would regard as radical renunciation. It is
in the practice of this type of giving — the offering of cheerful sacrifices — that we are most likely to discover the good
news of biblical stewardship impacting our lives.

How We Give

NOW I WOULD LIKE TO shift our focus somewhat to more
practical concerns. Thus far, I have concentrated on the
question of *why* we give money to the church and have suggested that faithful giving is of two types: 1) we support our
home congregation with contributions equal to our proportionate share of its budget expenses; and, 2) we answer
Jesus' call to renunciation by regularly giving away some of
our money in a way that goes beyond what would be a reasonable and obvious expectation of us. Now I wish to take
up the more practical question of *how* we give this money.

At one level, if we are faithful in giving to the church,
the question of *how* we make our gifts may not seem very
important. Indeed, if you feel that you are being faithful,
and if you have a system that works for you, then perhaps
you should just keep on with whatever it is that you are
doing. But, for others, I am going to suggest an approach

to giving that encourages faithfulness and that helps us
to understand what we are doing — and why. I recognize,
again, that those who need to grow in faithfulness on these
matters may find some of this daunting or discouraging
— but I hope that will not be the final verdict. The goal of
this approach is to move us out of the guilt-driven, manipu-
lative realm in which conversations about financial stewardship can so easily become mired, and move us into a
gospel orientation where we can feel good about our giving
and about how we are using our resources for God.

I recommend that we give money to the church in two
different ways, which I discuss under the headings *pledges*
and *offerings.* These terms are familiar to many churchgoers, but I use them to describe an approach that is different from common practice. In many churches today,
members are asked to make pledges regarding the total
amount of money that they plan to give to the church in
a year; I suggest that pledges be limited to one particular
type of giving only: proportionate support for the congregational budget. Further, in most churches today, members
fulfill their pledges by contributing to the offerings that are
collected at worship services; I suggest that offerings be devoted to something else: sacrificial giving that goes beyond
what we contribute as reasonable proportionate support.
Perhaps it will seem that I am complicating matters unnec-
essarily, but there are good reasons for setting the matter
up this way and, in truth, the program I am suggesting is
not very complicated at all.

❧ *Pledges*

I RECOMMEND THAT CHURCH MEMBERS make pledges
to their church that correspond to the first type of giving
discussed above: we should *pledge* to *support* our congregation with contributions that represent our proportionate
responsibility for its budgeted expenses. In doing this, we
are not being generous or making a sacrifice; we are being
responsible and fulfilling a basic commitment to the life
and mission of the community of which we are a part.

Our pledge will probably not represent everything that
we give to the church — it might represent only a small portion of what we give. Nevertheless, we need to fulfill that
pledge with contributions that are regular and dependable.
Payment of our pledge should not be affected by vacation
schedules or other anomalies. The church needs to be able
to depend on receiving this money from us regardless of
whether we are in town on any given week or whether we
overspent our budget on Christmas shopping.

Commitment to paying our pledge should also have
nothing to do with whether we are angry with the pastor or
disappointed with the congregation or frustrated by bu-
reaucratic maneuvers of the national denomination. We do
not give this money in order to influence church policies
or politics, nor do we give it because we approve of everything the church does. We give it because we are part of the
church and we *want* to belong to this fractious and flawed
family of God that is so beloved of Christ. John Westerhoff
tells about a time when his church adopted a new service
book and two members announced that they were going to

quit paying their pledges for as long as the new book was being used. A friend of theirs, who was also disgruntled, made an appointment to see Pastor Westerhoff and to the latter's surprise gave him a check equal to the pledges of the other two members. "I'll never like that book," the man said, "but this is family, and you don't vote with your *wallet*" (*Grateful and Generous Hearts,* p. 61). Such insight is necessary for the church to be the true people of God. Otherwise, the wealthiest members of the congregation (or at least those who pledge the most) would have undue influence in church affairs. And the poor (hypothetically those who pledge the least) might just be the ones who are richest in faith (James 2:5).

Ideally, I do not think that it is best to pay our pledge by putting money in the offering that is collected at worship services. There are better ways to pay it — better for practical reasons and also for religious ones. In our modern world, the absolute best way to pay a pledge may be through automatic fund transfers, so that the church receives whatever we have pledged directly into its bank account at the same time every month. The money is simply subtracted from our own bank account or, sometimes, taken right out of our paycheck — a modern equivalent for giving the "first fruits" of our produce (Proverbs 3:9). Many churches and financial institutions are now set up to allow for such a procedure. For those that are not, though, the next best way to pay our pledge is probably by writing checks on a regular basis and mailing them to the church in the same way that we would mail checks to cover other charges that we are responsible for paying each month.

Why pay a pledge in one of these ways? Because the offering that is a part of our Sunday morning service is not an occasion for fund-raising but a liturgical act of devout worship. It is a high point in the liturgy, a moment in which we are invited to offer sacrificial gifts to God out of love and thanksgiving and adoration. For me, the spiritual and theological meaning of the offering is lessened if I use it as an occasion for turning in my pledge payment which, to be frank, is not really much of a sacrifice.

This is not a terribly significant point, and if you can't follow me here, that's fine. Paying a pledge *is* one form of giving to God so there is certainly nothing wrong with making that a part of the offering on Sunday morning. But for me, personally, when I limit my pledge to fulfillment of what I consider to be my proportionate share of the church's budgeted expenses, paying that pledge becomes more of a basic responsibility (like paying bills) than offering a truly sacrificial gift of love. When I pay my pledge, I don't want to pretend that I am doing anything more than being a responsible church member, supporting the community of which I am a part. Pledging to support one's church and then paying that pledge (as promised) is a good thing to do, but it is not renunciation. Therefore, I recommend keeping pledges and offerings separate: mail checks or authorize fund transfers to insure that your church will regularly receive the support from you that is appropriate for its budget needs and your financial means. This is a duty. Perform it faithfully, and the offering can be a delight.

🌿 *Offerings*

I THINK THAT OFFERINGS SHOULD ideally correspond to the second type of giving we discussed above, to the cheerful sacrifices that are made by those who gladly renounce their possessions and give their money away in ways that go beyond what would constitute reasonable proportionate support for the congregational budget. This is an act of pure worship, an expression of deep faith, and a sure discipline for spiritual growth.

If we are paying a pledge to the church in the manner described above (an important *if*), then our offerings can be somewhat sporadic, spontaneous, unpredictable, and reflective of our varying levels of enthusiasm and areas of commitment. They can be spirit-led: we are free to follow our conscience and our intuition in deciding how much to give and when to give it. There is great joy in such giving, for we are not merely fulfilling a basic responsibility but, in truth, are opening our hearts to the goodness of God. It is in such giving that we become generous people. It is in such giving that we become grateful people. Indeed, it is in such giving that we become godly people.

The invitation to renunciation, to sacrificial giving, is an invitation to let the goodness of God take hold of us. God gives generously and graciously to all for one reason only — because God *is* good! And when we give to others in ways that go beyond what would be reasonably expected of us — when we give our money away for what seems like "no reason at all" — we do so because the goodness of God has taken hold of us. Life holds no greater thrill than this.

And there is no better place for such cheerful sacrifices to
be presented than within the context of a Sunday morning
worship service, as part of what we call "the offering."

I need to say, however, that our practice of sacrificial
giving need not be limited to gifts made to the church.
There are many other charities and good causes to which
we might want to make donations and, if we are paying our
pledges — providing our proportionate share of support
for our church's budget — then we may feel free to answer
Jesus' call to renunciation by giving to programs other than
the church. If I feel led to give that money to a college or
to a missionary society or to a health organization, or to a
homeless person on the street, that is entirely appropriate.
Indeed, I think there is a need in the present day for many
Christians to develop a sense of stewardship that points beyond the needs of the local congregation. Jesus called us to
be the salt of the *earth* and the light of the *world* (Matthew
5:13-14) and our devotion to matters of global concern may
constitute a fulfillment of that call.

Having said this, however, I can think of three reasons why it is often a good idea to devote at least some of
the money that we view as sacrificial giving (beyond our
pledge) to our local congregation:

First, the worship service itself is more meaningful
if we put *something* in the offering plate. This is a minor
point, more liturgical than economical, but I think that it
is always good to participate in the offering taken up at any
worship service by putting something in the plate that is to
be presented to God at the altar.

Second, just because we are doing our part in contributing proportionately to the church does not mean the budget will be met. There will be people in the congregation who do not give as they ought. There may be some with good intentions who due to unforeseen circumstances are not able to give as they wished. And there may be others who are ignorant of the church's needs or who are spiritually immature or just too stubborn to do what they should do. It doesn't matter: we are called to bear each other's burdens (Galatians 6:2). Some of us need to make up for those who don't give as they ought by giving *more* than our share — this is a simple reality.

And, third, there have probably been times in our lives when *we* were not contributing proportionately to the church. From a historical perspective, then, it seems entirely appropriate that we give more than our share now. I know that there have been times in my life when my participation in the life of a church community was sustained by the benevolence of others. Now, perhaps, it is my turn to provide such benevolence for someone else.

In any case, whether we make sacrificial offerings to our local church or choose to donate the money elsewhere, such renunciation bonds us not only to God but also to the network of interdependent human life of which we are only a part. John Westerhoff is fond of saying that we all live on an endowment. We are only able to have what we have and to do what we do because of *generations* of generous people who have gone before us. By appreciating what our forebears have done and leaving something for those yet to be born we can be in community with those who come after us — and with those who went before.

Discussion Questions

1. What do you make of this chapter's distinction between *support* and *sacrifice*? Is it helpful to think about our giving in terms of these two categories?

2. Do you have a fair understanding of what your proportionate share of support for your church's budget might be? Do you think that your current giving to the church is appropriate in these terms?

3. Do you know people who have moved "from reasonable to radical" and given their money in ways that go beyond what might be a usual expectation? Have you ever done this yourself?

4. What do you think of this chapter's suggestion that pledged support for the congregation be paid in a manner similar to "paying bills" (through automatic fund transfers or checks mailed to the church)? What are the advantages or disadvantages of people contributing in this way?

5. What do you think of the suggestion that the weekly offering be viewed as an occasion for making sacrificial gifts—over and above one's proportionate support for the church's budget? Would you be able to structure your own giving along those lines?

CHAPTER SEVEN

How Much?

What shall I return to the Lord for all his bounty
to me?

Psalm 116:12

THE WIDOW GAVE A PENNY (Mark 12:42); the Pharisees
gave a tenth (Matthew 23:23); Zacchaeus gave half (Luke
19:8); the rich man was asked to give all (Mark 10:21-22). The
early church shared everything in common (Acts 2:44-45;
4:32); Barnabas sold a field (Acts 4:37); Jesus' disciples left
their boats and nets (Mark 1:18, 20). How much will we give?

How much of our money should we give to the church?
Many churchgoers are hesitant to ask this question — and
I think I know why. To quote a song from the sixties, it often seems like when anyone
asks "How much should I
give?" all they hear is "More!
More! More!" This is unfortu-
nate — the church should not be a wellspring of guilt and
manipulation. Christians who are basically faithful to God
in matters of stewardship should be able to achieve a level

> 🎵 **How much**
> **will we give?**

of confidence that lets them feel good about their giving
and grants them immunity from the pleas and ploys of
those who always want to tell them, "It's not enough!" But
how much *is* enough?

※ *Tithing*

THE SIMPLE ANSWER THAT SOME books offer to the
question "How much should I give?" is, "Ten percent of
your income." That is the principle of *tithing* and a hand-
ful of biblical passages may be quoted to justify the expectation. In the Old Testament, Abraham gave a tenth of
the spoils he had won in a battle to the mysterious priest
Melchizedek (Genesis 14:17-20; see also Hebrews 7:4-10).
Jacob promised to give God one tenth of all the material
blessings he received (Genesis 28:18-22). In later times,
Israelites were expected to follow the examples of these
patriarchs by dedicating a tenth of certain belongings to
the support of the religious establishment or other designated causes. In actual practice, tithing underwent consid-
erable modification over the years, with changes regarding
which items were subject to the tithe, to whom the tithe
was to be paid, and to what use it should be put (see Leviticus 27:30-33; Numbers 18:20-32; Deuteronomy 14:22-29;
Nehemiah 10:32-39). The "one tenth" principle, however,
remained fairly consistent. In one especially memorable
instance, the prophet Malachi upbraided Israelites for
"robbing God" when they failed to bring their full tithes to
the temple in Jerusalem (Malachi 3:8-10).

Jesus appears to have supported tithing as an outward sign of righteousness, but he also criticized tithers for neglecting "weightier matters" of God's law (Matthew 23:23; Luke 11:42) and for adopting a haughty attitude of self-righteousness (Luke 18:9-14). In general, he seems to take tithing for granted as appropriate for the Jews of his day but wants to emphasize the transcendent principle of 100 percent stewardship (giving all to God by using everything as God would want).

The apostle Paul retains the basic notion of proportionate giving (2 Corinthians 8:3, 12-13), but allows for the specific percentage to be decided by the individual (2 Corinthians 9:7). He is also careful to say that giving should be voluntary and he insists that "if the eagerness is there, the gift is acceptable according to what one has" (2 Corinthians 8:12). Although he never mentions tithing specifically, it seems clear that he would have regarded tithing requirements as similar to other laws (sabbath regulations, dietary restrictions, and so on) from which Christ has set people free (Galatians 3:23-26).

Christian churches have adopted various attitudes toward tithing throughout history. In the present day, some churches portray tithing as a regulation that is binding upon all Christians just as it was upon ancient Israelites. Most churches, however, reject the idea of requiring any particular level of financial support, but continue to respect voluntary tithing as a noble ideal. In any case, the concept is not easily transferable to modern circumstances.

The first thing that I would want to say about tithing is that it should be related to the type of giving that we have called "sacrifice" rather than to that which qualifies as proportionate support for one's own congregation. In the Bible, what was given as a tithe was given *away,* used (most often) to support Levitical priests or (sometimes) given to the poor. Thus, the tithes were not typically used to support local congregations of which the tithers were participating members. The Levitical priests performed duties important to the religion of Israel, but they did not teach Bible studies, preach sermons, visit the sick, or catechize the young. By New Testament times, the synagogue (led by rabbis, not priests) had become the locus of spiritual fellowship and religious education for most Israelites. Tithes, however, were not paid to synagogues, and the money that one gave to support one's local synagogue (comparable to what is given to a local congregation today) would not have been construed as a portion of one's tithe. Thus tithing, if it is to be practiced today, should properly apply to gifts that we offer *after* we have made appropriate contributions to meet our local congregation's needs. Ultimately (as you will see), I don't much care whether people tithe, but I don't think there is any merit in allowing people to think that they are tithing when they are not. In biblical terms, tithing would mean giving away 10 percent of our income *over and above* what we give as responsible church members to support the life and mission of our local church community.

The matter gets even more complicated, however, when various questions of application arise: should Christians tithe on their "gross income" or "net income"? On their income before taxes or after taxes? The Bible offers little help with such questions because the passages in the Bible that deal with tithing envision a cultural and economic situation quite different from our own. Some have suggested that a literal institution of tithing would involve a greater hardship for persons in our current environment than it did for people in biblical times. The temple to which the tithe was usually paid in ancient Israel was both a religious institution and a political one. At least some of what was covered by the tithe in that context (for example, social welfare for the poor) might be covered by taxes in ours — and it is worth noting that the Israelites were never expected to give 10 percent of their income to the temple in addition to paying 33 percent to the government in income tax. Furthermore, there is no close analogy in our modern world for the arrangement that provided the primary rationale for tithing in biblical times: supporting a class of priests who were forbidden to own property or engage in agriculture.

Other points may be raised. In ancient Israel, most people lived freely in the land and built simple homes with their own hands. They were not saddled with mortgage payments or real estate taxes. They did not have to make monthly payments to the electric, gas, or phone companies. They did not have to maintain expensive health insurance policies. The social-economic systems of ancient Palestine and modern America are so different, some would say, that the "give away a tenth of your income" principle is no longer sensible. A more reasonable standard might be for the church to ask its members to give away one-tenth of their *disposable* income — in other words, the money that they have left after "necessary bills" are paid.

Personally, I think that all the reasons why tithing would be a greater imposition in our era than it was in biblical times need to be considered within the context of one inescapable fact: we live in a time of incredible affluence. Most Christians in America could give away a lot more than one tenth of their income (gross income, before taxes) and still be wealthy beyond the wildest dreams of Israelite farmers or Galilean fishermen. In biblical times, a wealthy person might own two suits of clothing (see Luke 3:11); an extremely wealthy person might own half a dozen. Today, a person with six nice outfits would not be considered rich, not by a long shot, and the Bible verse that says "if we have food and clothing, we will be content with these" (1 Timothy 6:8) seems so quaint as to sound almost ridiculous. Who would be content with just food and clothing — even if it was a *lot* of food and clothing?

In biblical times, tithing was a standard expectation for common people. The rich would be deemed stingy if they did not give much more (cf. Luke 19:8). Jesus said, "From everyone to whom much has been given, much will be required; and from the one to whom much has been entrusted, even more will be demanded" (Luke 12:48). Thus, it is not surprising to find experts on stewardship today who conclude that tithing is simply too easy for Christians in an affluent society like ours.

For others, that just seems idealistic. John Brackett observes that "for most people today, the idea of giving away ten percent of their income seems financially impossible and psychologically incredible: why would anyone choose to give away *that much money* — to the church or to anyone else?" (*On the Pilgrim's Way: Christian Stewardship and the Tithe,* p. 2). For one thing, people grow accustomed to affluence and do not think of themselves as wealthy. We come very quickly to think of possessions as necessities rather than luxuries, and if tithing would require conspicuous limitations on our lifestyle then it strikes us as an extravagant expectation that would only be fulfilled by persons who are exceptionally generous. A goal for saints, perhaps, but not for everyday folk like us.

Where does this leave us? I think that it is impractical and unwise for the church to insist on tithing as a *requirement* for Christians in the modern world. For one thing, there are just too many problems with transference of context for us ever to figure out exactly what the analogous expectation ought to be. Beyond that, and more important, the Bible as a whole encourages a gospel-oriented approach to stewardship that emphasizes cheerful expressions of faith and praise rather than potentially grudging fulfillment of requirements (2 Corinthians 9:7). It would not be too difficult, furthermore, to come up with a list of people for whom tithing could be inappropriate if not irresponsible: those who live on a fixed income in an inflationary economy; those who are strapped with high medical bills; those who are overwhelmed by high-interest debt; and so on. The Bible also teaches, for instance, that we ought not give religious institutions money that is needed for the care of dependent family members (Mark 7:9-13; 1 Timothy 5:8).

Nevertheless, the basic idea of regular percentage giving remains compatible with biblical thought, such that some concept of a tithe may appropriately be regarded as a "traditional benchmark" or "worthy goal" for Christians who find it useful to conform their voluntary giving to some external standard. Having such a standard can help us to ground our good intentions in habit rather than mood, and to guard those intentions from the inevitable vicissitudes of piety.

We should also note that millions of Christians in the world today testify that they do practice tithing and do not find this burdensome. Luther Powell says,

> Tithing has been tested thousands of times in the laboratory of human experience. What is the verdict? With very few exceptions, people who have tried tithing heartily recommend it to others, and they, themselves, have no desire to give it up. . . . To the tither, it simply becomes a natural thing to do. It fits into religious life like prayer, public worship, and personal witness. . . . Many things in life have to be experienced to be understood and appreciated. Being a Christian is like that. So is tithing. (*Money and the Church,* pp. 226-27)

And L. David Brown says simply, "I have never met an unhappy tither" (*Take Care: A Guide for Responsible Living,* p. 62).

I suggest, then, that we think of tithing (however it is defined) as a *traditional guideline* for Christian giving, a standard that many Christians find to be appropriate and attainable. I do not want to assume, however, that tithing is a realistic goal for everyone, and I do not believe the church should exploit the principle in ways that make people feel bad about their chosen level of stewardship. In particular, tithing should never be presented as some sort of timeless requirement expressing what God demands of all people everywhere.

Before going any further let us pause to remember a basic concept that I hope undergirds everything in this book. I indicated at the outset (page 4) that the Bible contains more *promises* regarding stewardship than *requirements*. It would be easy to lose sight of this right now because, in this chapter, we seem to be talking a lot about what God expects of us. But let's not forsake the gospel orientation. What the Bible says about stewardship is good news, and within the context of the gospel what at first appear to be expectations are often revealed to be possibilities — *options, not requirements.* With regard to tithing, for instance, the best question to ask is not "Do I have to give 10 percent of my income to the church?" The answer to that question is simply, "No." A better question to ask may be, "Would I like to be the sort of person who is spiritually and financially able to give 10 percent of my income to the church?" And if your answer to *that* question is "yes," then there is a good chance that tithing is for you after all.

> ⁑ **Within the context of the gospel what at first appear to be expectations are often revealed to be possibilities.**

With this in mind, I will now present my own formulas for figuring how much to give. They don't work out quite as neatly as some may hope; this is a matter for intuition and prayer, not just arithmetic. Nevertheless, in approaching this question I try to build on the foundation of what has been said in this book thus far. The issue of "how much to give" actually entails two different concerns, for faithful giving is of two different types: support and sacrifice. It helps, I think, to consider the two separately and to ask two distinct questions. First, we may ask about the proportionate share that we should be expected to contribute to the life and mission of the church of which we are a part. Then, we may ask about our willingness to go beyond this in offering cheerful sacrifices to God.

❦ A Fair Share

THE FIRST QUESTION TO ASK is *How much do we want to pledge for the support of our church?* We want to do this as responsible church members. Making such contributions does not constitute generosity; it merely fulfills a basic commitment to our community of faith, allowing us to do our part to support the congregation of which we are a part. Such contributions are always voluntary, as they should be, but not to make them would usually be irresponsible.

As for the amount that we should contribute, the basic biblical principle that applies here is *proportionate giving.* The Bible teaches that giving is to be "according to means," so that there will not be relief for some and pressure on others (2 Corinthians 8:3, 11-13). As the apostle Paul says, "It is a question of a fair balance." This principle obviously applies to income: persons who have more money are generally expected to make larger contributions than persons who have less (cf. Luke 12:48). Giving expectations, however, should also be proportionate to one's circumstances, which are a little more difficult to determine. A single parent with four children should

🐦 **How much do we want to pledge for the support of our church?**

not be expected to contribute the same amount as an individual with an identical income but no dependents. There is no exact science for determining the relative financial standing of all the various members of a church, but rough estimates may be possible and such estimates are all that is necessary.

In an ideal situation, I think that a church's pastor or financial secretary will help members determine their appropriate support level for proportionate giving to the congregation. As I indicated above (pages 133-34), churches that take this matter seriously may invite members to submit financial information to some trained personnel who will then be able to provide approximate guidelines for what the members' expected levels of responsibility may be. But even with a minimal amount of information, you may be able to come up with an estimate on your own. Here is a simple procedure for getting a rough idea of what your proportionate share of support for your church might be:

1. Get the bottom-line figure for the church's total annual budget. This information should be readily available in congregational reports, but if you have trouble finding it, ask the pastor or some other church leader.

2. Ask what the total number of "active giving units" for the church would be. Stewardship experts use the term "active giving units" to refer to individuals or families who provide realistic financial support toward meeting the congregation's expenses. For convenience, they often define an "active giving unit" as an individual or family who gives more than $100 to the church in a year. The figure then includes minor givers, but excludes those whose contributions are so slight or sporadic that they cannot really be counted on in terms of meeting budget needs. In most churches, the number of active giving units will be a smaller figure than the number of persons who attend church on Sunday morning — not all of those persons can be counted on to provide support. The realistic number you need to know is, "How many active giving units contributed more than $100 to our church last year?"

3. Divide the budget total by the number of active giving units. This will give you a median figure for what a person or family of average income and average circumstances should be expected to contribute to the congregation in a given year.

4. Now, here's where the real guesswork comes into play: try to determine your financial position among the congregation's committed givers. Do you think that you have about as much money as others whose life circumstances are similar to yours? Do you have considerably less or considerably more? Don't obsess over trying to figure this out to an exact amount — just estimate roughly whether

your financial posture seems to be about average, below average, or above average. Then, adjust your proportionate responsibility for expenses accordingly. As I indicated, this is not an exact science, but if your congregation does not offer you any assistance in figuring out such matters, you just need to do the best you can and assume that the figure you come up with represents a faithful guess regarding the amount that you should pledge.

As I have said previously, this advice for determining your pledged support to your local congregation goes against the grain of what most stewardship experts today are teaching. Many will claim that it is theologically problematic or spiritually deficient to tell people to give *to* a budget rather than *from* their hearts. The amount of our giving should not be determined by budget needs but by the goodness of God that takes hold of us and transforms us within. I actually agree with the experts on this point, but it need not run counter to what I am proposing because we are not done yet. Pledging to support our local congregation with contributions that are appropriate to our proportionate share of the budget is not all there is to financial stewardship. It is, rather, a starting point, a first step toward faithfulness that brings us to a point of basic responsibility.

So what should you do if you figure your pledge in the manner described above and come up with an amount that seems exorbitantly high — far more than what you are currently giving, and more than you feel that you are able to give? Well, now, you at least know that others in the church have been giving more than their due in order to make up for your lack. That may be disheartening news but, personally, I think that knowing the truth about such matters is better than not knowing it. And now, perhaps, you can do something about it. Do *not* pledge more than you will actually be able to contribute. Rather, set a goal for increased giving that you think is realistic and let that be your pledge for this year. Keep to it, even if it is nowhere near what it ought to be, and try to increase it again in the future. And don't feel too bad: most of us have been there, at one time or another. This is how the church works — we bear each other's burdens, and we do so gladly. Look forward to the day when you are able to give more than your share, making up for others who will be in the position that you are in now.

🎔 *A Cheerful Sacrifice*

THE NEXT QUESTION TO ASK IS *How much might we give in offerings that represent a cheerful sacrifice for God?* We want to do this as joyful followers of Jesus Christ whose hearts are alive with love and gratitude for God. Making these contributions *does* constitute generosity; it is giving in the fullest sense, giving that goes beyond what mere common sense would suggest as appropriate for supporting our church community.

The basic biblical principle that applies here is *renunciation.* Jesus calls us to give up our material possessions as a cheerful sacrifice to God: it is an act of worship; it is an expression of our faith in God; and, it is a spiritual discipline that bonds our hearts in love to God and allows the love of God to take hold of us. Thus, there can be no "correct way" for determining the amount that any particular individual ought to give away. Such giving is spirit-led and the amount can be sporadic and spontaneous. Still, many Christians find it helpful to develop some sort of plan that will help them to fulfill their good intentions and to evaluate their progress toward a stated goal.

🐦 How much might we give in offerings that represent a cheerful sacrifice for God?

I will suggest two different formulas for setting such a goal. Which of these appeals to you may be a matter of temperament, for the first is somewhat mathematical and the second, completely intuitive.

The mathematical formula invokes the principle of tithing, which we have already discussed. You might decide that your goal will be to give away one-tenth of your money over and above what you give to the church as your share of support for its budgeted expenses. There is good biblical precedent for doing this and millions of Christians have demonstrated that it is possible to fulfill such a goal in a way that is not burdensome but a spiritual delight. As for whether "one-tenth of your money" means one-tenth of your gross income or net income or disposable income, it really makes no difference. The standard is an arbitrary one anyway, far from an exact emulation of what anyone was actually practicing in biblical times. The point is simply to have a guideline for measuring one's giving, and stating that goal in terms that can somehow

---

🦃 **Giving in an Age of Affluence:**

How Much Do We Need?

As a young man, John Wesley reportedly earned thirty pounds at his first job; he kept 28 pounds, and gave two away. Later, when his salary had doubled, he still kept 28 pounds but now gave 32 away. Eventually, he was earning 120 pounds, still living on 28 and giving away the rest. Wesley's motto regarding finances was, "Gain all you can, save all you can, give all you can."

Many Christians today live in affluence, possessing far more than they need. Prosperity is a good thing, but we must weigh our surplus against the needs of those who are in want. John Westerhoff says that when he considers the needs of the poor compared to his own relative afflu-ence, the question becomes not "What do I need to give?" but "What do I have a right to keep?"

Jesus tells a parable of a rich man who dresses in purple linen and dines sumptuously while a poor beggar lies at his gate (Luke 16:19-31). The point is not that there is anything sinful about eating good food and wearing nice clothes, but to do so without a care for the one in rags and hunger is simply perverse (on this, see also James 2:15-17).

---

be construed as "a tithe" is liturgically and traditionally appealing.

A second formula is quite subjective. We are trying to figure out how much to give as a cheerful sacrifice over and above our proportionate support for our church's budgeted expenses. Accordingly, we may find it helpful to evaluate our giving prayerfully in light of the two words *cheerful sac-rifice*. These words can provide us with twin guidelines:

- If our giving is not a *sacrifice*, we are probably not giving enough.

> Jesus says that this rich man would have known better if he had "listened to Moses and the prophets." Moses said to love your neighbor as yourself (Leviticus 19:18). The prophets got more specific, rebuking those who lived in luxury while others dwelt in poverty (Amos 6:1-6).
>
> What should Christians do? Those who are affluent must listen to Moses and the prophets and to Jesus as well. They must search individually and as communities for the balance between enjoying the material blessings God has bestowed and sharing this bounty with the neighbors they are called to love.
>
> Each must make up his or her own mind (2 Corinthians 9:7), but this advice from Scripture may be a guide:
>
>> As for those who in the present age are rich, command them not to be haughty, or to set their hopes on the uncertainty of riches, but rather on God who richly provides us with everything for our enjoyment. They are to do good, to be rich in good works, generous, and ready to share, thus storing up for themselves the treasure of a good foundation for the future, so that they may take hold of the life that really is life (1 Timothy 6:17-19).

■ If we are not giving *cheerfully,* we may be giving too much.

Let's take the second point first. Yes, it is possible to give too much. We sometimes set goals that are unrealistic. We have some idea of what we would really like to be able to do and we commit ourselves to doing this. Setting such challenges is generally good, but if the giving becomes burdensome to the point that we regret ever having made such a commitment (to God or to the church or simply to ourselves), it may be best to pull back. God does not want us to give out of compulsion or a sense of guilt.

Nevertheless, our cheerful giving *is* to be a sacrifice. The purpose of offerings that go beyond pledged support for the church's budget is renunciation, and such giving is most meaningful when we can actually feel its effects. If we merely give out of our surplus, donating money that we will never miss, the experience of sacrifice can be lost. We want to experience in some real way the absence of what we have given up.

In Old Testament times, care was taken to insure that offerings to God represented a genuine sacrifice on the part of the Israelites. When farmers offered an animal as a sacrifice they were to pick from the best of their flock or herd as opposed to sacrificing one of the defective beasts that wouldn't have been good for much anyway (Deuteronomy 17:1; Malachi 1:6-8). Later, when David sought to buy a threshing floor as a place for setting up an altar for God, the owner of the threshing floor offered to give it to him for free, with a number of animals (for the sacrifices) thrown in as well. David was taken aback by this offer and insisted on paying for everything. He proclaimed, "I will not make offerings to the Lord my God that cost me nothing!" (2 Samuel 24:24).

Over the years, I have heard many testimonies from people who have made sacrificial offerings of their material goods. The *most* meaningful of these often come from people who gave up something that they would have valued — a vacation, perhaps, or a special purchase (see above, pages 59-60). In such cases, the *sacrifice* aspect of the gift comes noticeably to the fore in a way that is clearly felt by the giver. And yet, the people who made these gifts did not regret their decisions to give up whatever it was that they would have valued. In keeping with the apostle Paul's advice, they made up their minds to do these things and they did not do them "reluctantly or under compulsion" but with glad and generous hearts. They made the sacrifices *cheerfully.*

How much money you give away in a spirit of renunciation, over and above your pledged support for your church's budget, is a personal matter. It is a matter for your own prayers and your own conscience, but your goal might be to give enough that you will experience the loss of what you gave as a genuine sacrifice and yet as one that you will be glad to have made. You should not give such offerings simply because you think you have to, or even because you think you ought to. Rather, let the goodness of God take hold of you and, then, give because you *want* to.

🏵 Good News

GOOD NEWS! YOU CAN BE a generous person! The plan that I outline above is manageable for most people in most churches today. If it does not seem so to you, then let the gospel of biblical stewardship break into your life and transform your too-typical conceptions.

Most people in most churches today are financially able to contribute appropriately to their church's budget and to give sacrificially beyond that 10 percent or more of their income. They are able to do so cheerfully and still have more than enough money to enjoy life with full appreciation for the pleasures that God's good creation (and modern conveniences) afford. If that level of giving seems outlandish to you — completely beyond reach — it may be because your current habits and patterns were not developed with faithful stewardship or generous giving in mind. If

⤵ **You can be a generous person!**

that is the case, set new goals and let God lead you toward them: *growth* in giving is what is often most important and most faithful stewards can attest to having surprised themselves repeatedly by attaining and surpassing goals that once seemed unobtainable. And if the goals themselves seem more radical than reasonable (what sane person would give away *that* much of their money?) you may still be conformed to thinking as this world thinks. The good news of stewardship is that God is capable of renewing our minds (Romans 12:2), transforming us to envision life with remarkably different and eminently more satisfying perspectives and priorities.

It is more blessed to give than to receive (Acts 20:35). When you become a truly generous person, you will know the joy that living as a faithful steward brings. By way of summary, let us mention a few sample aspects of that joy.

First, there is the joy of realizing that everything we are and everything we have belongs to God. Generous, sacrificial giving serves as a constant reminder of this. We give away a significant portion as representative of our commitment to give 100 percent to God by using all as God would want. Such offerings are symbols that take hold of us — we cannot usually give away our money without really meaning it — and so the commitment runs deep and truly affects us at every level. We come to live in an almost constant awareness that we are but stewards, that God is the owner and master of all we are and all we have. Why is this good news? It is good news, in part, because it inculcates the values of trust and gratitude, driving out the pettiness of envy and greed, and moving us beyond anxiety to that precious secret of contentment that the apostle Paul knew (Philippians 4:11-12). It is also good news because, quite frankly, God is much better at running our lives than we are: it is *liberating* to learn that we are not ultimately in charge. We have a creator, we have a redeemer, we have a sustainer. We are only stewards living under the rule of God, yielding to the lordship of Christ, listening for the guidance of the Holy Spirit.

Second, there is the joy of loving God and of expressing that love through sacrificial gifts that demonstrate our praise and adoration of the God who is so good to us. The Bible speaks of believing in God, serving God, and obeying God, but above all it speaks of *loving* God. Indeed, Jesus designated *this* as the first of all the commandments: "Love the Lord your God with all your heart and with all your soul and with all your mind" (Matthew 22:37). It seems crass to link love with money, but there is nothing crass about saying we demonstrate love by sharing — even by giving up — that which is precious to us. And Jesus also said that the love of mammon is diametrically opposed to the love of God (Matthew 6:24). So, we express our love for God when we take generous portions of our money and give it away, cheerfully and sacrificially. We not only *express* our love; we *increase* it. In some mysterious way what we do with our treasures actually affects our hearts such that the cheerful sacrifice bonds our hearts to God and helps us love God more. Generous, faithful stewards typically have hearts overflowing with love for God and the joy of the Lord becomes their strength (Nehemiah 8:10).

Third, there is the joy of pleasing God and of receiving the rewards and blessings that God promises to bestow upon us. "Well done, good and faithful servant," is the word spoken often to trustworthy stewards in the parables of Jesus (for example, Matthew 25:21, NIV). They are the words every Christian longs to hear. Merely knowing that we have done as we ought should be reward enough (Luke 17:10) and yet our Lord assures us that there will be more (Matthew 6:3-4; Luke 6:38; 1 Corinthians 3:14; 2 Corinthians 9:6, 11). We do not know exactly how such rewards will be presented, or when, or whether they will be tangible or spiritual, but we do know that God is faithful to every promise of Scripture. Those who give up their belongings will enjoy blessings they might not have received otherwise.

Finally, there is the simple joy of benefitting others with our gifts. We do not always see the benefit — money cannot always be given to causes where there are immediate and obvious consequences. But we can know that the world will be a better place because we did not squander the opportunity to be generous. This world is not always beautiful or kind, but consider what it might be like without benevolence. How many hospitals and universities and art museums exist today as a result of generous patrons? How many diseases have been cured? How many souls have been saved? How many hungry children have been fed? And how many individuals and communities have benefitted from the simple, continued presence of churches where God is glorified and the gospel of Jesus Christ proclaimed in word and deed? Our gifts *do* make a difference and knowing this can be a constant and legitimate source of gladness for those who give them.

You can be a generous person and live in this joy as one who knows God, loves God, pleases God, and benefits others. I invite you to accept God's invitation to generosity, to *live* as one who belongs to God and to *give* as one for whom giving is a duty and a delight.

Discussion Questions

1. What do you think about tithing? Do you know people who tithe? Have you ever done so yourself?

2. How would you personally answer the question posed on page 161: Would you like to be a person who is spiritually and financially able to give ten percent of your income to the church? Why?

3. Follow the suggestions on pages 163-65 to determine a rough estimate for what might be your proportionate responsibility for contributing to the support of your church. How does this compare with your current level of giving?

4. Have you ever had the experience of making cheerful sacrifices in the manner described in this chapter (pages 170-71) — giving in such a way that you "feel the loss" and yet do not regret making the gift?

5. As you reflect back over this book, what are the principles of *good news* that you want to keep with you? How will your life be different if the goodness of God takes hold of you and shapes you into a truly generous person?

Some Suggestions
for Further Reading

Blomberg, Craig. *Neither Poverty Nor Riches: A Biblical Theology of Material Possessions.* Grand Rapids: William B. Eerdmans, 1999.

Blue, Ron, with Jodie Berndt. *Generous Living: Finding Contentment Through Giving.* Grand Rapids: Zondervan, 1997.

Brackett, John K. *On the Pilgrim's Way: Christian Stewardship and the Tithe.* New York: Office of Stewardship (The Episcopal Church), 1988.

Brattgård, Helge. *God's Stewards: Theological Study of the Principles and Practices of Stewardship.* Translated by Gene J. Lund. Minneapolis: Augsburg, 1963.

Brown, L. David. *Take Care: A Guide for Responsible Living.* Minneapolis: Augsburg, 1978.

Carlson, Martin E. *Why People Give.* New York: National Council of Churches in Christ in the U.S.A., 1968.

Childs, James M., Jr. *Greed: Economics and Ethics in Conflict.* Minneapolis: Fortress, 2000.

Clinard, Turner N. *Responding to God: The Life of Stewardship*. Philadelphia: Westminster, 1980.

Cross, Marie T. *The Price of Faith: Exploring Our Choices about Money and Wealth*. Louisville: Geneva, 2002.

Cunningham, Richard B. *Creative Stewardship*. Nashville: Abingdon, 1979.

Grant, F. C. *The Economic Background of the Gospels*. New York: Oxford University Press, 1926.

Grimm, Eugene. *Generous People: How to Encourage Vital Stewardship*. Nashville: Abingdon, 1992.

Hall, Douglas John. *The Steward: A Biblical Symbol Come of Age*. Revised edition. Grand Rapids: William B. Eerdmans, 1990.

Hinze, Donald W. *To Give and Give Again: A Christian Imperative for Generosity*. New York: Pilgrim, 1990.

Hoge, Dean R., et al., *Money Matters: Personal Giving in American Churches*. Louisville: Westminster John Knox, 1996.

Johnson, Douglas W. *The Tithe: Challenge or Legalism?* Creative Leadership Series. Nashville: Abingdon, 1984.

Kantonen, T. A. *A Theology for Christian Stewardship*. Philadelphia: Muhlenberg, 1956.

Kauffman, Milo. *Stewards of God*. Scottdale, Pa.: Herald, 1975.

Lane, Charles R. *Ask, Thank, Tell: Improving Stewardship Ministry in Your Congregation.* Minneapolis: Augsburg Fortress, 2006.

MacArthur, John. *Whose Money Is It Anyway?* Nashville: Word, 2000.

MacNaughton, John H. *More Blessed to Give.* Revised edition. San Antonio: Episcopal Diocese of West Texas, 1983.

Powell, Luther P. *Money and the Church.* New York: Association, 1962.

Reumann, John. *Stewardship and the Economy of God.* Grand Rapids: William B. Eerdmans, 1992.

Roop, Eugene F. *Let the Rivers Run: Stewardship and the Biblical Story.* Grand Rapids: William B. Eerdmans, 1991.

Schneider, John R. *The Good of Affluence: Seeking God in a Culture of Wealth.* Grand Rapids: William B. Eerdmans, 2002.

Thompson, Rhodes. *Stewards Shaped By Grace: The Church's Gift to a Troubled World.* St. Louis: CBP, 1990.

Thompson, T. K., ed. *Stewardship in Contemporary Theology.* New York: Association, 1960.

Tournier, Paul. *The Meaning of Gifts.* Richmond: John Knox Press, 1963.

Vallet, Ronald. *The Steward Living in Covenant: A New Perspective on Old Testament Stories.* Grand Rapids: William B. Eerdmans, 2001.

Vincent, Mark. *A Christian View of Money: Celebrating God's Generosity.* Scottdale, Pa.: Herald, 1999.

Vischer, Lukas. *Tithing in the Early Church.* Translated by Robert C. Schultz. Philadelphia: Fortress, 1966.

Werning, Waldo J. *The Stewardship Call.* St. Louis: Concordia, 1965.

Westbrook, Kay. *Enter into the Joy: Stewardship as a Way of Life.* Boston: Daughters of St. Paul, 1996.

Westerhoff, John H. *Grateful and Generous Hearts.* Atlanta: St. Luke's, 1997.

INDEX OF SCRIPTURE REFERENCES